**Winner of the DuSable Museum Award
for
Excellence in Poetry**

"I have read and thoroughly enjoyed *Earthquakes and Sunrise Missions* especially "the Women" poems. Your handling of Black women in your poetry continues to inspire and offer hope."

Sandra E. Gibbs
Director, Special Programs
National Council of Teachers of English

"Dressed in the format of poetry dividing beginning and ending essays, *Earthquakes* addresses the need for and purpose of the written word as a function of language as a transmitter of culture, from a clear and precise social/political perspective. An exciting new work by one of the most widely read Black poets on the scene today."

The Black Collegian

"A significant and overdue work from the poet-activist from Chicago. Mr. Madhubuti is one of the few poets out of the Black tradition who is not afraid of ideas or controversy."

The Buffalo Challenger

"*Earthquakes and Sunrise Missions* is one of those books that you have trouble with because you don't want to put it down...but the cover gets ragged from daily wear; the poems are so close to home, you want to make your agreement known, people catch you mumbling to yourself. In fact this book "makes you want to holler 'right on' and throw up both your hands."

The Final Call

"*Earthquakes and Sunrise Missions* should be an easy apparatus to aid the Black critic in finding his people's ear. It is a strong book of truths, which will not be added to the library to collect dust, or go 'out of style'...but will serve as a handbook of reference guide to the common denomination of Black life, Black love, and the destiny of Black people.'"

Cora L. Guinn
The Houston Defender

"The thrust of Madhubuti's writing has only intensified over the years. It has perhaps, even taken a rather scholarly turn as he moves the message from poetry to essays and critical analysis. His words have not lost a bit of its relevancy or timelessness...Instead, it has become more firmly stated and finely crafted."

Denise Carreathers Armstrong
Contemporary Black

"A more muted Madhubuti, tempered by time but no less poignant, writes forcefully about challenge, despair, rebuilding and most importantly, about love for those of the diaspora. A Highly appropriate book for sociological studies of the African American experience.

Vivian V. Gordon, Ph.D
Associate Professor of Sociology
University of Virginia

EARTHQUAKES
AND
SUNRISE MISSIONS

POETRY AND ESSAYS
OF BLACK RENEWAL
1973 - 1983

the word is
that the women & the men
will love again,
families will reappear
& children playing and growing
will be commonplace
& contiguous.

BOOKS BY HAKI R. MADHUBUTI [Don L. Lee]

POETRY:
Think Black
Black Pride
Don't Cry, Scream
We Walk the Way of The New World
Directionscore: Selected and New Poems
Book of Life
Earthquakes and Sun Rise Missions

CRITICISM:

Dynamite Voices: Black Poets of the 1960's

ESSAYS:

Enemies: The Clash of Races
From Plan To Planet, Life Studies: the Need for Afrikan Minds and Institutions
A Capsule Course in Black Poetry Writing
        Co-authored with Gwendolyn Brooks, Keorapetse
        Kgositsile and Dudley Randall

ANTHOLOGY:

To Gwen With Love
        Co-edited with Pat Brown and Francis Ward

RECORDS:

Rappin and Readin
Rise Vision Coming
        with the Afrikan Liberation Arts Ensemble

EARTHQUAKES
AND
SUNRISE MISSIONS

By Haki R. Madhubuti

Afterward By Darwin T. Turner

Illustrations By Calvin Jones

Third World Press, Chicago, Il

Revised
First Edition 1984   Third Printing December 1987

ISBN: *0-88378-108-5*   [*cloth*]

0-88378-109-3   [*paper*]

With gratitude to Bobbie Womack and Larry Crowe for their unselfish help in the production of this work and to Darwin Turner and Calvin Jones for their support and encouragement. To the National Endowment for the Arts and the Illinois Arts Council for their support in helping to make this book a reality.

Manufactured in the United States of America
Third World Press, 7524 S. Cottage Grove Ave., Chicago, Il 60619
(312) 651-0700

DEDICATION

For Bringers of the Future

Safisha Madhubuti

Assata Shakur   *Lu Palmer*   *Frances Cress Welsing*

Herbert Daughtery   *Inez Hall*   *Bobbie Womack*

Gil Noble   *Janet Sankey*

The Institute of Positive Education Family

all transforming confusion into wisdom,
hardships into challenge,
struggle into meaningful work,
weakness to steel.

———— IN REMEMBRANCE ————

Hoyt W. Fuller
Robert Hayden
Richard Adisa Humphrey, Jr.
George Kent
Bob Marley
Willie Melvin, Jr.
Larry Neal
Walter Rodney
Mbembe Milton Smith
Bobby Wright

*the good die prematurely
  often in battle
  at war
  always at the firing line
  in the midst of complicated confusion
  doing good
  cutting into concrete,
  challenging mediocrity
  ever
  contributing wisdom and
  example
  to those they loved

  their people.

Contents

THE MEN

Also By Haki R. Madhubuti (Don L. Lee)

Poetry
Think Black
Black Pride
Don't Cry, Scream
We Walk The Way of the New World
Directionscore: Selected and New Poems
Book of Life
Earthquakes and Sunrise Missions
Killing Memory, Seeking Ancestors

Criticism
Dynamite Voices: Black Poets of the 1960's

Anthologies
Say That The River Turns
To Gwen, With Love
(co-edited with Pat Brown and Francis Ward)

Essays
Enemies: The Clash of Races
From Plan To Planet, Life Studies:The Need for Afrikan Minds and Institutions
A Capsule Course in Black Poetry Writing
(co-authored with Gwendolyn Brooks, Keoraptse Kgolsitsile, and
Dudley Randall)
Kwanzaa: A Progressive and Uplifting African-American Holiday
*Black Men: Obsolete, Single, Dangerous? The Afrikan American Family in
Transition*

Records and Tapes
Rappin' and Readin'
Rise Vision Coming
(with the Afrikan Liberation Arts Ensemble)
Mandisa
(with the Afrikan Liberation Arts Ensemble)

Prefatory Note

Earthquakes and Sun Rise Missions is my first book of poetry since **Book of Life** which was completed in 1972 and published in 1973. A missing decade for a poet is unusual. Included here are the poems that thundered out between three books of essays and other work. In this volume I have delicately positioned two essays that begin and end the work, providing the poetry with a cultural and literary context to dance in. Words cut and heal. I am not a doctor, however I would like to think that **Earthquakes and Sun Rise Missions** is preventive medicine.

HRM

First Edition 1984
Third Printing December 1987
Fourth Printing 1990

ISBN: 0-88378-108-5 [cloth]
0-88378-109-3 [paper]

With gratitude to Bobbie Womack and Larry Crowe for their unselfish
help in the production of this work and to Darwin Turner and Calvin Jones
for their support and encouragement. To the National Endowment for the
Arts and the Illinois Arts Council for their support in helping to make this
book a reality.

Manufactured in the United States of America
Third World Press, 7524 S. Cottage Grove Ave., Chicago, IL 60619

Poetry: A Preface

Poetry will not stop or delay wars, will not erase rape
   from the landscape,
will not cease murder or eliminate poverty, hunger or
excruciating fear. Poems do not command armies, run
school systems or manage money. Poetry is not
intimately involved in the education of psychologists,
physicians or smiling politicians.

in this universe
the magic   the beauty   the willful art of explaining
the world & you;
the timeless   the unread   the unstoppable fixation
with language & ideas;
the visionary   the satisfiable equalizer screaming for
the vitality of dreams   interrupting false calm
demanding fairness and a new   new world are the
poets & their poems.

Poetry is the wellspring of tradition, the bleeding
connector to yesterdays and the free passport to
   futures.
Poems bind people to language, link generations to

each other and introduce cultures to cultures.
Poetry, if given the eye and ear, can bring memories,
issue in laughter, rain in beauty and cure ignorance.
Language in the context of the working poem can
raise the mindset of entire civilizations, speak to two
year olds and render some of us wise.

To be touched by living poetry can only make us
        better people.
The determined force of any age is the poem, old as
ideas and as lifegiving as active lovers. A part of any
answer is in the rhythm of the people; their heartbeat
comes urgently in two universal forms, music and
poetry.

for the reader   for the quiet seeker
for the many willing to sacrifice one syllable mum-
blings and easy conclusions
poetry
can be that gigantic river
that allows one to recognize
in the circle of fire
the center of life.

Introduction

**BLACK WRITERS AND CRITICS: DEVELOPING A
CRITICAL PROCESS WITHOUT READERS**

There may not be a need for Black writers and
critics or a Black critical process in the next twenty-
five years. I do not wish to shock you, but as a
working writer, publisher, editor and teacher for most
of the last twenty years, my observation is that I do
not see book buying or borrowing high on the priority
list of Black people. To put it more emphatically,
reading (or research and study) as a necessary life
enrichment experience is not foremost in the **must do**
list of most Black people. And I must say that this
issue of a non-reading people may be the most
dangerous contributing factor in our misdevelopment
over the last twenty-five years in this country.

Let me be more specific. Even though there is a
greater percentage of Black high school graduates
within the general population in 1982 than there was
in 1962, this does not mean that the basic life support
skills (reading, writing, computation, and critical
thinking) have increased accordingly within the Black

community. Indeed, all this actually says is that more Black people are **involved** in an "education" or "training" process. The negative results of that process are not being debated openly. In fact, if one looks at the educational system of a city like Chicago, what is common knowledge is that its 2.5 billion dollar educational machine is actually turning out many Black students who not only cannot read or write, but even more serious, is producing young men and women who actually fear and hate books. This is to say, after twelve years of what has been loosely described as "education," the great majority of Black students would have serious difficulty reading and writing themselves into the lowest level civil service jobs. However, the most dangerous aspect of this is that the educational process, which is built upon the ability to **decipher** and **use language**, has for the most part developed in Black children not only a severe dislike for books, but also ingrained into their psyche is a disrespect for reading and writing as **required** intellectual processes. In any kind of society this is unacceptable, but in a highly scientific and techno-logical one it is absolutely frightening.

We need to be honest about this. As a person who is intimately involved in writing, editing, pro-ducing and distributing books and other educational materials, I find this state of affairs quite exasperating. Many people dwell on the failure of the sixties and seventies. We are asked almost daily "What happened to the Black revolution?" Those of us who continue to chart a course of self-reliance are openly laughed at and patronized. Black Studies as a serious discipline, with the exception of a few universities, is lifeless or has been redefined into ethnic or minority studies. whereas the study of Native Americans, Asians, Hispanics, and women is given priority over the study of 30 million people of Afrikan descent in the United

States. To say that this was not expected is to do an injustice to our best minds.

The Black Consciousness movement was destined to falter, was programmed to encounter hills and valleys—not due to the legitimate ups and downs of instituting a serious discipline of study, but because its very founding was grounded in political reality and activism and at its inception its stated objectives were dangerous. For above all else this movement chose to question the position of Black people in America and the world.

We all know that the development of a consciousness of self within any people, first and foremost, deals not only with the identity of said people—nationally and internationally—but also speaks to the powerfulness or powerlessness of that people. Those serious Black Studies and Afrikan Studies departments that did not self-destruct due to confusion, poor funding and lack of vision represented an important intellectual base for the whole Black Consciousness movement. Those men and women were not only about the business of questioning power relationships between Blacks and whites, but were also extremely concerned about the complete alterations of these relationships for the best interest of Black people. "But Haki, we know all of this," you may say, "What does this have to do with Black writers and critics and the development of a Black critical analysis?" What I am saying is that there will be no serious need for Black writers, critics, editors or publishers if Black people are not reading—that is if, as I believe, Black people represent our primary audience. And to be perfectly frank, a culturally serious and literate Black public does not exist within our national group to the degree that one does for Japanese, Jews and Anglo-Saxons.

There continues to be a concerted effort nationwide to de-educate Black people or at a minimum undereducate us. The education of Black children is not priority among whites or **Blacks**. There are many reasons for this, but it is obvious that we have become overly concerned with integrating rather than educating.

There is little if any long range thinking or planning in process in the area of Black skill development at a mass level that would prepare us for the 21st century. Unlike other ethnic groupings in this country—the Black elite does not see service to the Black majority as something they wish to be involved in, not only because there are few "tangible" rewards, but this is not something they've been **taught to do**. Therefore, that generation that participated in the struggle of the fifties and sixties has by in large left the struggle and is serving the same governmental and corporate structures that it so "righteously" fought against. That backward move has been devastating.

Mass Media and the Rape of Serious Consciousness

Other than the rapid disolution of the Black family unit, one of the greatest weapons used against the development of a Black literacy and consciousness, in my estimation, has been the mass media— specifically television. There are more televisions in Black homes than telephones. Blacks as a group watch more television than any other people in this country—somewhere on the average of 4 to 6 hours a day. The films, recordings and radio industries have contributed to our lack of development, but to a lesser degree. However, it must be noted that the average high schooler in Chicago is more frequently seen with a cassette tape or radio under his/her arms than books.

In a special "Black Books Bulletin" issue on communications, Lu Palmer, the noted communicator, stated that "...the institution of mass communications is the most awesomely powerful force in our society...this is true because the media of mass communications are the vehicles which transmit messages, images and symbols into the minds of people...and people act, react and behave as a result of what they believe." Communication is the transmission of ideas, of information from one unit to another. Television, radio, film, newspaper and magazines represent mass communications and that is "An institution.....which is the arm of a political-economic-racist structure which is designed to maintain and perpetuate control over people."

I am sure you have noticed that in defining mass media I did not mention books, quarterlies or journals where much of the serious discourse takes place. The Black readers of "Black Scholar"; "Black Books Bulletin", "Freedomways", "Western Journal of Black Studies", "First World", "New Directions", "Yardbird Reader", and other serious Black and non-Black material are a significant few. The hard fact is that the majority of Black people don't read anything other than the Bible, television guides and record charts, "True Confessions", girlie magazines, astrology and dream books, racing forms, and other related materials. We receive most of our information by way of television. In a very important book, *Four Arguments for the Elimination of Television*, the author, Jerry Mander states;

> The average household has the set going more than six hours a day. If there was a child, the average was more than eight hours. The average person was watching for nearly four hours daily. And so, allowing eight hours for sleep and eight hours for work, roughly half of the people in

this country were watching television even more than that.

As these numbers sank in, I realized that there had been a strange change in the way people received information, and even more in the way they were experiencing and understanding the world. In one generation, out of hundreds of thousands in human evolution, America had become the first culture to have substituted secondary, mediated versions of experience for direct experience of the world. Interpretations and representations of the world were being accepted as experience, and the difference between the two was obscure to most of us.

He goes on to discuss the development of artificial environments and the across the board acceptance of secondary interpretations of reality:

Thus far, political theorists have failed to make very much of the effect our modern environments have on us. Failing to grasp that the physical world we live in is itself arbitrary, and thereby likely to be confusing to masses of people who seek solid ground on which to stand, political observers have not made some critical deductions. Primary among these is that when people cannot distinguish with certainty the natural from the interpreted, or the artificial from the organic, then all theories of the ideal organization of life become equal. None of them can be understood as any more or less connected to planetary truth. And so the person or forces capable of speaking most loudly or most forcefully, or with some apparent logic—even if it is an unrooted logic—can become convincing within the void of understanding.

In which you program a situation where:

...that if you control environment carefully enough, you can shatter all human grounding. This leaves the subject in such a disconnected state, you can easily predict and control how he or she will respond to the addition of only one or two stimuli.

Indeed, this is the case if we carefully survey the Black community where we are still crowded and boxed into carefully prescribed areas, where the contact to family and friends is restricted by design, where there is little, if any, noticeable constructive production of any kind; where human sharing is not encouraged; where individualism and isolation is pushed as the norm and where most natural experiences are either frowned on or are openly put down. The best example of the latter would be the lack of breast-feeding among young Black mothers who are encouraged to use artificial milk not only because it is readily available and aids the economic sector, but breast-feeding will, we are told, affect the firmness of the mother's breast, thus affecting her female sexuality. The question of the real reason for the breast is never asked—whether it exists as a sexual artifact or as a functional organ in the life process of Black babies?

The object of course of mass media is to **sell America.** To make you buy products and services you not only do not need, but under natural circumstances would never have thought of as existing, e g., vaginal sprays, electric toothbrushes, or elevator shoes. Therefore television, which is the most sophisticated system of negative advertisement, acts more as an agent of "anti-experience" and contributes generally to the dulling of "human sensibility" and "dims awareness of the world." Mander states that television, by focusing people on events well outside their lives, "encourages passivity and inaction, discourages self-awareness and the ability to cope personally..." Television

> encourages separation: people from community, people from each other, people from themselves, creating more buying units and discouraging organized opposition to the system. It creates a surrogate community: itself. It becomes everyones intimate advisor, teacher and guide to appropriate behavior and awareness. Thereby, it becomes its own feedback system, futhering its own growth and accelerating the transformation of everything and everyone into artificial form. This enables a handful of people to obtain a unique degree of power.

Where does this leave the writers and critics? I'm afraid in pretty bad shape if part of our purpose is to write and interpret the literature for Black people. Of course this smacks of outright elitism if by design only the priviledged few among our people can read, or are involved in the analytical process. This is why serious development is multi-faceted, and why as we seek alterations in the political system, the educational apparatus needs to be watched; as we confront the military industrial complex, we also need to work toward transformation of the economic system; and as we hit all of them we need to realize how we are all being manipulated by mass culture at its most sophisticated levels. (Also see Mankierwicz and Swerdlow, **Remote Control: Television and the manipulation of American Life**].

Indeed it has been stated that, "literature is a social institution, using as its medium language, a social creation. Such traditional literary devices as symbolism and metre are social in their very nature.

They are conventions and norms which could only have arisen in society. But, furthermore, literature represents life," and "life in large measure, is a social reality, even though the natural world and the inner or subjective world of the individual have also been objects of literary imitation." White writers, being an integral part of this society, are accorded a certain elite station within America, usually an honor station, whether they challenge the system or not. His or her rewards are fame, money, and for many, a certain amount of security.

However, the Black writers, no matter how talented, are viewed as outsiders—no matter how hard they try to get in. That is, the western literary world does not revolve around whether Ismael Reed or Toni Morrison are publishing this year; the publishing establishment is not overly concerned if a Gwendolyn Brooks leaves Harper and Row; the emerging publishing conglomerate will not blink an eye over the fact that the early works of John A. Williams are out of print. In fact, Black writers, regardless of how they are accepted by the white reading public, are at best talented tokens. If Gayl Jones and Ntozake Shange (and Black women writers are in now) did not ever publish another book, they would not be missed by the so-called white literary world. At best Black writers have been used and tolerated, but not respected.

On the other hand, the Black critic within the white editing world has not faired much better. In fact none of the major white book reviewing media such as New York Times Book Review, Saturday Review, New York Review of Books, Commentary, Book World, Publishers Weekly, Library Journal and Los Angeles Times Book Review recognize any Black literary critics as authorities of Black literature. Our best critics, George Kent, Addison Gayle, Jr., Eugenia

Collier, Hoyt Fuller, Darwin Turner, Stephen Henderson, Peter Bailey, Carolyn F. Gerald, and Shirley Anne Williams are not called on by any of the major media to deal with Black writers published by the major white publishing houses. However, of those critics mentioned, none of them, to my knowledge, is losing any sleep over this fact. If one studies the criticism and works of these critics there is one common thread that flows through their production—there is a sincere love for the written word. Also, within that group the level of cultural sensitivity and literary competency is beyond question. Addison Gayle, Jr., in his important work **The Way of The New World,** states that "The critic, the cultivator of the soil in which the best ideas might be nurtured, like the novelist must possess a pervasive grasp of his subject, must know the landscape, the valleys, the hedges, highways, and byways of the human soul. Only such knowledge enables him to evaluate the work of others." Gayle continues in reference to the fiction form, "The novel is the one genre which attempts in dramatic and narrative form to answer the questions: what are we and what is it all about?...These are social questions. They comprise such an essential part of the makeup of the novel that the evaluation of such novels requires an understanding of the social, political and historical forces which produced them."

The Black Critic

Part of the function of the Black critic is to locate the wisdom and the inconsistencies in the writer's work. The Black critic is also a resource that if understood and used properly would not only promote the literature, but aid the writer in finding his people's ear. The critic should also bring to the reading public as well as to the writer, an understanding of world literature—especially how it relates to Black people. Mari Evans in a very important essay* divides Black literature into three phases:

1. Literature of Celebration and Instruction
   a) Afrika   b) diaspora (early)
2. Literature of Encounter
   a) Asia   b) Europe   c) Caribbean, Central and South America   d) North America
3. Literature of Affirmation
   a) 1919—Harlem

Within her field of vision she brings clarity to the connections between "creativity, colonization and the artist as voluntary and involuntary part of the fabric." She feels that especially in North America where the "oppression" is most structured, most comprehensive and most unremitting "that the critic has a responsibility to examine the 'relationship of oppression to creativity." Without a doubt this is key—however we must also keep in mind that the critic has undergone the same "oppression" and this too will affect his or her vision. However, the examination must be done.

Creativity or the act of creating as a "normal" reaction to human involvement in the world is largely destroyed among many people in this society at an early age. I do not believe that I need to argue this point. However, for the few who are able to break-light with originality—poetry, novels, photography, etc., need to question if their work is an affirmation and not merely a reaction to secondary and negative stimuli. The critic needs to be involved in definitions: what is a racial consciousness? If the Black critic cannot supply the answers, we writers are again left to our own energies and alien influences that often confuse and misdirect the reading public.

* "The Nature and Methodology of Colonization and Its Relationship to Creativity" By Mari Evans, *Black Books Bulletin*, Spring, 1979.

Here are some suggestions for Black critics to consider:

1. We must deal with the written word in a historical, cultural, political and aesthetic context. We must not let our feelings for or against a writer cloud our assessment of his or her work.

2. We need to be well grounded in the Black way of life—not only well versed in the literature but also in the support systems—i.e., Black family life, Black music, Black spirituality, Black folklore, Black entertainment, etc.

3. We need to seek a new honesty—that is, rather than push mainly our ideas in the criticism of a work—we need to **really deal with the author's work. If we have battles to fight, don't hide behind someone else's efforts.**

4. We need to be open to experimentation of all types: ideas, concepts, philosophies. We need to be well versed in World literature, e.g., Afrikan, European, Asian, American, etc.

5. Black critics need to talk and listen to each other. They need to meet privately and discuss among themselves their own pitfalls and shortcomings, as well as innovations and new truths.

6. **We need to continue questioning our own standards**—what is needed is clarity and direction as well as a focus on that which is good. Also remembering that a bad first novel or book of poems does not necessarily mean that one cannot write—it may mean that the writer needs direction, special attention and encouragement.

7. The critic also needs to be a fighter and **visionary**. Black critics are creators also. Addison Gayle in **The Way of the New World**, Shirley Ann Williams

in **Give Birth to Brightness,** George Kent in **Blackness and the Adventure of Western Culture** and Darwin Turner in his many books, are also taking part in the creative process. The critics, as creators, fight the battles and recognize the War.

8. Promote life-giving and life-saving change—and this is done in part through the promotion of writers who are dealing with ideas and directions that are beneficial for a liberated or oppressed people.

9. To understand that for an oppressed people all work is political whether the author meant it to be or not. A part of the critics' responsibility is to aid in the decolonization process. That the art of writing is not a **neutral art for art's sake hide away process.**

10. The critic, along with the publisher and writing institutions, must establish a means of rewarding and recognizing the contribution of Black writers. There needs to be an annual recognition feast—not where Black authors fight each other for the prize of the year, but a sincere attempt made to honor the progressive contributions of young, mid-stream and older writers. As **The Autobiography of Miss Jane Pittman** picked up all of its television Emmys—few realized that the author was a Black man. The John A. Williams, Angela Jacksons, Gwendolyn Brooks, John O. Killens, Ernest Gaines, James Baldwins, Amiri Barakas, John H. Clarkes, Paule Marshals, Mari Evans, Alice Walkers, Sonia Sanchezes and others need to be publicized and their works pushed with the same vigor and force that a new record by Stevie Wonder or Earth, Wind & Fire is pushed. Black

publishers, editors, and critics need to come together and establish a way of saying thanks to our writers.

11. Black critics, along with teachers and parents, need to be involved in community reading programs. This is where the material needs to be pushed. They need to be emphasizing the **Joy and Adventure of Reading.** I can honestly say that one of the changing points in my life was when at fourteen mother handed me a copy of **Black Boy** to read.

12. Help Black writers get published. Write letters to editors, get involved with all aspects of publishing. Not only bring a critical eye to the writers but also to editors, publishers and others in the book industry.

✳ In conclusion, I feel that the Black critic must resist becoming an imitation white critic or all-knowing guru of the universe. However, he or she must go beyond just developing a theory of Black literature, beyond killing each other over the ultimate definition of the Black aesthetic. As difficult as it is, the Black critic must discourage cliques and personality cults. Shirley Ann Williams in her timely and important work, **Give Birth To Brightness,** sets forth what I feel is the ultimate and enduring role of the Black critic:

> Our most important function, however, lies in examining the works of our writers to see how well they present their versions of Black life, even if those versions are not our own, to see what insights they are trying to reveal to us, to see if they have reworked the old stereotypes and themes and images to bring us more understanding of ourselves as individuals and as a group of fragmented, oppressed people. We are, then, not translators of meaning, but interpreters

who refract image and situation, plot and metaphor, character and symbol, illusion and theme through our knowledge and study of the history and cultural expressions of Black people, through our personal experiences, in order to add another voice to the developing conversation between Black writers and Black people. And our collective voice will have its own distinct tone, its own unique information to impart.

Our approach to knowledge, especially the written word, should be at the same level of seriousness that we approach lovemaking and war. Remember that the only places in the western world where large quantities of "pertinent" knowledge (information) is stored are in government, educational, military and corporate computerized data banks and libraries (books). Black people, en masse, do not have free and unlimited access to the data banks, and our accessibility to libraries and books is automatically and seriously curtailed as the Black generation that does not respect the written word increases. The old saying that "the best way to hide something from Black People is to put it in a book" is fastly becoming reality. We are fighting for the minds of our people as well as the just development of the world. Just think of the possibilities if all high schoolers before graduation had to study and digest the works of Richard Wright, Gwendolyn Brooks, Sterling Brown, Chester Himes, Margaret Walker, Langston Hughes, M. Karenga, Sonia Sanchez, Lerone Bennett, Kalamu Ya Salaam, Sam Yette, Chancellor Williams and others. What would be the results of that? That's our mission, if we believe in the future of Black people. We must develop not only a literate generation but a politically and culturally aware one too. Reading is a major life developing requirement.

General knowledge doubles itself about every six years and scientific knowledge doubles every two to three years—there are approximately 34,000 books published in the United States each year and an unbelievable number of specialized magazines, scholarly journals and monograms. Also newsletters and special interest papers flood the mind. The United States may not be the most literate nation in the world, but it certainly has more information available to the general public than any other nation. The great majority of the information that is freely circulated goes untouched by our community either because of ignorance or non-concern. The need for a highly literate and analytical mind to deal with today's world is not a priority with us. The respect for books, the search for knowledge, the reverence for great minds and the commitment to intellectual development is not as important as basketball or hair styles. And, until our priorities change, we will not be able to compete or complete our task.

Black critics must not only analyze but must legitimize the Black writers' work and also aid in making their work available to the Black community. To the mothers and fathers—on special days (and not so special days) buy your child a book instead of candy or toys. When birthdays come around, introduce our children to the beauty of words. Limit television and comic books. To do less speaks of death in its most lasting form—the slow but efficient erosion of the mind; a **mindless** people are without question an enslaved people. A mindless people are a people that join rather than initiate, obey rather than question, follow rather than lead, beg rather than take. To allow this state of affairs to continue is indeed a serious and profound comment on the state of our literacy.

Haki R. Madhubuti

and if there is time
wait
measure stillness
and quiet,
redo moments of
kindness and if
there is misunder-
standing change
yr words and
come again,

ISSUES AND KILLING
TIME

The Petty Shell Game

with raped memories and clenched fists. with small thoughts and needless time we indulge in destruction bathing ourselves in comedy and fraudulent posture:

willa mae is going with big daddy t and lula is pregnant and don't know who the father is, cleavon said that the father is "we the people."

quite a profound statement among losers and people beaten into the gutter and like desperate rats continue to destroy with:

richard g. is a faggot and pretty johnny is bald under that rag on his head, rev. jones is going with sister mary & sister emma & sister sara & but

the important issue here always, especially among the young is

where is the party this weekend &

where you get that boss smoke, man?

yet, as the hipped whipped often say, "only fools work" not daring to take into consideration that "fools" built the western world and raped the rest of it. yes, "only fools work" as we non-fools every early monday morn   fight each other for position outside the state welfare department.

Message

& if there is time
wait
measure stillness and quiet.
redo moments of kindness
& if there is misunderstanding
change yr words & come again.
We can do what we work to do.
slaves have children,
drive tanks,
visit playboy clubs, buy
$60 ashtrays and get extremely
angry at children leaning against their
cars.
Wait.
yes, there is time for love   but
equal & often more moments must be given to
war.
& even within this madness
special seriousness must be
got to be allocated for the
children

We can do what we work to do
measure stillness and quiet
noise is ever present.
if we are not careful we will not
hear the message
when it
arrives.

Expectations

people Black and stone
be careful of that which is designated beautiful
most of us have been taught from the basements
of other people's minds.
often we mistake strip mining for farming
and that   that truly glows is swept under
the rug of group production.
it is accepted in america that beauty is
thin, long, & the color of bubble gum.
few articles generated by the millions are beautiful
except   people.

trust people
one by one
the darker they come
the more you can give your heart,
their experiences most likely are yours
or will be yours.
even within the hue & hueless
among them are those
who have recently lost their
ability to recall.

they can hurt you
drop you to your knees with words
much of that which blast from their mouths
is not them   the offense is
they do not know that it is not them
as they rip your heart open
and reduce you to the
enemy.

The Writer

in america the major reward for
originality
in words, songs, and visual melody
is to have dull people
call you weird
while asking what
you do for a living.

Everything's Cool: Black America in the Early Eighties

in middle, rural, urban & combative america
it is a laborious challenge to explain racism and
   oppression
to a people that have among their members a
materially comfortable leadership and a complacent &
ignorant middle class that eats regularly, wears de-
signer socks, ventures into debt at will, lose themselves in artificial stimuli, are extraordinarily mobile &
largely expect the serious rewards of life in the next
world.

freedom is often confused with owning cars & bars
and being able to cross state lines without passports.
functional knowledge (e.g., computer technology,
producing food, governing self) is measured in one's
ability to quote the evening news & pontificate for
days on the merits of astrology or star power as it
relates to Black struggle. to many the haitian crisis
is a new dance, el salvador is mexican food, south
afrikan apartheid is a media creation and the only
foreign policy that is crucial to their lives is the paris
contribution to the yearly ebony fashion fair.
liberation on the real side is possessing the capacity
to swim in self pleasure & mundane acquisitions
without negative comment or challenge.

this cool crowd
believes that the majority of Black people suffer
because they are either lazy, unskilled, not motivated
or unlucky and that color & previous condition of
slavery is not germane to their current living status.
to quietly suggest to them that most of our people
exist in a state of dispirited boredom & wrecking
poverty only confirms their "lazy or unlucky" theory &

is accepted as a comment on the deficiencies of the
Black poor & have little to do with other people
and their economic & political systems. this
mindset is wide spread among all cultures in america
& for poets or anyone non-white to issue reminders
is considered rude and "sixtyish" & is to be
construed as a note on one's own inability to "make
it" in the main stream of the melted dreams.

the conscientious doer is labeled disrupter & is
perceived as an economic failure (the only kind that
counts) and one's words fall on blown out ears
& pac-man mentalities. the prevailing beliefs in the
land encourage individuals, families, corporations,
and police departments to pursue their most
outlandish desires; representing an understatement of
acute confusion, where cultural and traditional values
are lost to the latest fads & electronic games.
it is clear and crystal
that the one
undeniable freedom
that **all** agree exist
for Black people in america
is the freedom
to
self destruct.

The Secrets of the Victors

(the only fair fight is the one that is won)
Anglo-Saxon Proverb

forever define the enemy as less than garbage,
his women as whores & gutter scum,
their children as thieves & beggars,
the men as rapist, child molestors & cannibals,
their civilization as savage and
beautifully primitive.

as you confiscate the pagan's land, riches & women
curse them to your god for not being productive,
for not inventing barbwire and DDT,
perpetually portray the **natives**
as innocent & simple minded while eagerly
preparing to convert them to **your way**.

dispatch your merchants with
tins & sweets, rot gut & cheap wines.
dispatch your priest armed with
words of fear, conditional love and
fairy tales about strangers dying for you.
dispatch your military
to protect your new labor pool.

if there is resistance
or any show of defiance
act swiftly & ugly & memoriable.
when you kill a man
leave debilitating fear in the hearts of his
father, brothers, uncles, friends & unborn sons.
if doubt exist as to your determination
wipe the earth with his
women, girl children & all that's sacred;
drunken them in bodacious horror.

upon quiet, summon the ministers to
bless the guilty as you publicly
break their necks.
after their memories fade intensify the teaching.

instruct your holy men
to curse violence   while
proclaiming the Land Safe
introducing
the thousand year Reign of the Victors
as your Scholars
re-write the history.

Is Truth Liberating?

if it is truth that binds
why are there
so many lies   between
lovers?

if truth is liberating
why
are people told:
they look good when they don't
they are loved when they aren't
everything is fine when it ain't
glad you're back when you're not.
Black people in america
may not be made for the truth
we wrap our lives in disco
and sunday morning sermons
while
selling false dreams to our children.

lies
are refundable,
can be bought on our revolving
charge cards   as
we all catch truth
on the next go round
if
it doesn't hurt.

The Shape Of Things To Come
(December, 1980—what some people do to themselves is
only the first chapter in what they will do to others)

in naples, italy
the earth
quaked and three hundred thousand are
without beds, toilets and knowledge
of loved ones.
hourly revisions enlarge the dead & injured.
normal shortages exist adding
burial coverings
for the young
(evidently falling into the earth by the thousands is
not punishment enough)
the word goes out
to the makers and shapers of sordid destinies
that
"this is the time to make the money"
immediately
quicker than one can pronounce
free enterprise
like well oiled rumors   or
elastic lawyers smelling money
plastic coffins appear
& are sold at dusk behind the vatican
on the white market.
in italy in the christian month of eighty
in the bottom of unimaginable catastrophe
the profit motive endures
as
children replenish the earth in
wretched abundance.

Beirut Massacre
(September, 1982)

rejecting with contempt
will not get it,
will not conceal sabra and shatila.
whispering histories of bibical cities
does not excuse bulldozing of bedrooms
did not stop
babies and mothers screams
as bullets sliced their heads.

this is a lesson in creating pure,
pure hatred.
this is the secret of how
to erase memories of great crimes.

rejecting with contempt
is watered paper against self-righteous
christians spitting lead or
jews opening flood gates of fire.
contempt for horror
does not protect the unborn,
old and crippled from worms, or
from underground insects in armed pants
raging for land and vengeance.

Negro Leaderships

our leaders are manufactured
in up state new york in nobackbone field
just outside the catskills
on the yes plantation.
most are conceived with fools gold
in their teeth & jelly beans in their
thinking units & slide out of the incubator
**dancin doin the rump the charlie charlie bump
the rump the knee bends the crawl but but up**
their palms are greased with pig's oil &
automatically turn upward when near money.
they define their interest identical to that
of the major diamond & gold producers in the world.
negro leaderships share more than a need for greed
most have rusty knees, purple tongues & dry lips.
sport pot bellies, sore buttocks, & manicured toe nails
& excrete waste frontal.
**get it leroi step willie do the rump rump shuffle
now tongue out   eyes big   spread yo butt now**
they are trained at the best divinity schools,
do not spit verbs, read secular materials or
ponder too deeply about the negro problem.
black theology is blasphemous
& they view the world's enemy as
atheistic communism, scientific humanism &
thinking black women.

taught from birth 101 ways to say
no
to the realities of their people
the only value that
lights their fire
is
women bearing gifts,

an upward turn in the money market and
invitations from the mayor to march
in the annual st. patrick's day parade.

THE WOMEN

dark women are music
Some complicated well worked
rhythms
others simple
melodies.

Women Black: Why These Poems.

to see her is to realize why man was made different. is to realize why men were cut rough & unready & unfinished. the contrast would be like a magnet. and we fell into each other like wind with storm, like water into waiting earth. this woman black, this unbelievable wonder, would test the authenticity of a man's rough. a rap of beautifully rhymed words would not work with her. a well rehearsed smile on the good side of your face, or that special gleam from under your tanned shades could not penetrate this woman black. even the whole of you, in your pants tight with life did not cause undo motion in her.

woman means more than woman
more than brown thighs
black lips, quick hips &
unfounded rumors
more than the common, more than the rational &
irrational, more than music, more than rough stones

& unread books, more than keepers of the kitchen, more than berry black, mellow yellow, & town brown, more than quick pussy, more than european names followed by degrees, more than nine to five order takers, more than fine, more than fox evil eyes big legs tight hips or women of the summer.

this is why i write about you. i want to know you better. closer. so this is my message to you. not a study. not a judgement or verdict. just observations and experiences. a lifestory, specifically the last sixteen years. above all poems of **love** going against that which is mistakenly passed off as **love**. this is a collection of intense feeling and complete touch. these are poems that were not ripe or ready for earlier books. these are poems that had to come to you in their own time, their own color & meaning. i have tried to do you justice in all of my works, but this Woman of the Sun, is the real test of my seriousness & dedication to you. my mother & her mother are here. my father's mother is here. my sister is here. the women black that i have loved & loved & loved & still love are here. my wife, quietly, as is her way, travels throughout these pages. this is the work that i slept, ate and travelled with. this is the beginning & middle the over touched, with memories from arkansas to michigan. this is an inadequate gift to the other half of me, and to the whole of you. the you that often goes unnotice, unheard, & unthanked. the you that is lost is in the power plays of men and life.

woman black
i have tried to write about you
words

in a language strange & not of our making
words
refreshingly new
clean, lively, honest & uncomplicatedly indepth
words
forging & fighting their way into meaning
knowing too that
words
are like people are like you
woman black
& if left to simple interpretation
could be twisted, misused & misunderstood.
i will write about you with loving care
my woman
this is my pledge to you for already
there is too much confusion surrounding
someone as wordless as
you.

loved one this is a tribute to the beauty and strength
of you, a comment on the good & bad of you, a
commitment to the inside & out of you, a confession
to the limited understanding of you, an appreciating
love note to the intricate you. lady love sixteen years
of you are here. over a decade of joy, struggle, hurt &
growth. you have brought meaning & purpose to my
life, have connected me to the tangibles & moved me
beyond the rhetoric of ideas to the necessity of
deeds. this is my testimony to you who have taught
me & my comeback to those of you i have failed.
please know that i have tried & will continue to go
against **whatever** for & with you. finally, these poems;
these words say as much about me as they do about
you. there are no real spaces separating us. **we are
one. believe it.** believe in it. women. **women of the
sun.**

MATURITY

emma jean aged one night
back in september of 63'
it was after them girls
had received death in alabama
on their knees
praying
to the same god,
in the same church,
in the same space,
she prayed.

she aged that night
after the day had gone
and left her with her thoughts.
left her with the
history of her people in
america.
emma jean matured that night
and knew that in a country
that killed the children
under
the eyes of **their** god   that
she nor her people
were safe.

emma jean
decided back in september of 63'
that she would let her people
know that they were not safe in
america
this is what she has done
and is doing   if she has not found you
look for her   kiss & hug her
thank her and then help her
to help us
mature.

ABORTION

she,
walla (queen) anderson
miss booker t. washington jr. high of 1957,
miss chicago bar maid of 1961
had her first abortion at 32
after giving birth to
john (pee wee) jackson at 14,
mary smith at 15 and a half,
janice wilson at 17,
dion jones at 19,
sara jones at 21,
and
richard (cream) johnson at 27.

on a sun filled day
during her 32nd year
after
as many years of aborting
weak men who would not stand
behind their own creations
she
walla (queen) anderson
by herself   alone   without consultation
went under the western butchers
to get her insides
out.

Safisha

1

our joining into one proceeded like
sand through a needle's eye.
slow, bursting for enlargement & uncertainty.
a smoothing of passion and ideas
into spirited permanence and love.

there are decades of caring in you,
children loving that makes the father
in me active and responsible.
you forecasted the decline of marble shooting
& yo yo tricks, knowing too that hopscotch
& double dutch could retard early minds if
not balanced with challenges and language.

you are what brothers talk about
when serious & commited to loving life.
when examples are used to capture dreams
you are that woman.
for me you are summer at midlife,
daring spirit and middlenoon love
and the reason i return.

2

dark women are music
some complicated well worked
rhythms
others   simple melodies.
you are like soft piano
black keys dancing between
& not becoming the white.
you bring dance & vision into our lives.
it is good & good
to be your
man.

Winterman

janice was winter
she had been made cold by
years of maltreatment rough years
of loneliness and false companionship
and now in the middle of her time
she refused to ever take another chance with a
blackman.

janice cursed the race. didn't see no good that black
people ever done. raised on a plantation where her
father was a sharecropper she watched her mother, in
her twilight years, steal away to jesus. the bible was
more than solution, more than heaven after earth, it
was food and water. it was ideas and values steeped in
fear and peaceful salvation.

janice ran north at twenty and between her twenty-first
and twenty-seventh year visited every store front church
on the west and south sides of chicago. she now
fashions herself a true missionary of the living gospel.
her mission was to save black men from the evil ways.
she wanted black men to be like mr. golding, the
husband of the white woman she did day work for. mr.
golding took care of his family, had a big house and ate
dinner with his family every night that he didn't have to
work late (he worked late at least twice a week).

most black men thought janice was fine but foolish.
after loving her many would brakelight fast. disappear
most leaving without an explanation. it came out later
that some of them didn't like being preached at at the
point of sexual climax. others felt that she prayed too
much and were uncomfortable with being compared to
judas. after as many men as churches janice in her

thirty-fifth year decided to close her legs and like her mother give her life, completely and unshared, to the only man in her life she declared had never failed her. jesus would now be the only man in her heart. it is not known exactly when during that year she was called but rumor has it that the **ultimate light** touched her the day after billy william, her last lover, started seeing her best and only friend minnie lou turner.

janice cursed the race. didn't see no good in black people. she turned slavishly and slowly toward her employers and began to live in. arlington heights, illinois was clean, peaceful and few black people lived there.

it was winter and windy
it was cold and white   and
jesus,
sweet, sweet jesus
was her man.

Bright Seasons, Coming

this woman you can rest with
can
relax with beyond rainbows and careful watch
this woman is special and special
gentleness within beauty.
she does not need the street lights
of lost weekends   or
unsilent phones to confirm herself.

she radiates peacefulgivings and calm winds
she is counted among the few
who
without effort or forethought,
without strangulation of space or time
circulates in motions that please
her man.

this woman of brown colors,
dateless ease & precious grace
is not vacant or unreachable,
is not wishful or ordinary temptations,
is not on attacks or retreats
but is
waterclear and well taught
(the rumor has it that her mother, grandmothers
and aunts talked to her during rained in evenings)
this woman of dark images
dresses in soft greens & sunrise oranges,
studies statistics,
afrikan nationalism & natural healing.
she reads sekou toure,
the doonesbury classics and
puts to memory the poetry of ntozake & zinzi mandela.
quietly and often, with her man,

loves to the music of keith jarrett and
pharoah sanders.

there are few streams in her neighborhood
yet
she is riverlike and springlove.
the men that were and are not now
remember her as
waterclear and oceandeep
remember her as
glowing   glowinglover   illuminating
bright seasons, coming.

Women Without Men

what of the women without men?
the energy within them
and
the life between their legs
will not dry up,
will not become desert absent of water.
do not ask these women   nights lonely
to forget
the days & nights of love
do not ask them to account for
the men passed,
forgotten and
unforgettable.
they do not control the lives
of their men.

their men are not theirs
their men are not themselves.

do not force these women
into religions
to hide behind words invented by men
ashamed of their own bodies.
religions
that cut their insides out
drain the passion and emotion from them
making them cold liquid
running from life
like
fire from water.

the women without men
feel the energy within them
and know that their fire

will not dry up,
will not become desert absent of tomorrows.
know this and urge them
to seek their missing lives
wherever the beauty.

Ad in a New York Weekly Newspaper

Lesbian: "In New York City
alone, estimates H Johnson of the
Committee for the Visibility of the
Other Black Woman, "there are a few
thousand black lesbians." And three
and a half million women. All of whom
are invited to a forum on Black Lesbian
Sexuality exploring such singular topics
as the Untouchable Bulldagger, Sexual Dys-
function (lesbians have problems, too), Aides
and Techniques (demonstrations of Ben Wa Balls
and vibrators), and Fantasies (obsessed
with riding a wild tiger?). There'll be sex
therapists, psychologists, university
professors, and Lady Diane, who promises an
erotic dance. Passion punch, breast cakes,
herbal aphrodisiacs. Women only.
October 18 at 6, Harlem State Office
Building, 163 West 125th Street, $6, 565-000 (Lhitcraft)

like me
if u don't know what
Ben Wa Balls, breast cakes & herbal aphrodisiacs
are
& not "obsessed with riding a wild tiger"
consider yrself   (in this order)
an unhipped, country raised (anywhere outside NYC)
non-european educated farmer
& quite possibly a 20th century
cowboy hat wearin "dumbhead" who is,
contrary to popular belief,
absolutely
normal and sane.

Lovepoems

1

lately
your words are drugged passages
with razor edges
that draw blood & tears
    and
memories of less difficult moments
when   love
that beautiful   overused   emotion packed commitment
charged the body.
love
momentarily existed
actually transformed us
defying the odds
flourishing   enlarging us
if only for seconds
seconds that were urgently expected
and
overneeded.

2.

there are rumors afloat that love
is ill.
intimacy at best is over night
clashes
and morning regrets.
are
bodies underwashed in strange bathrooms
as lovers
& others   bang the door
softly running.
steppin cautiously in cracked silence

to spread rumors   that
love
is a diseased bitch
deserving death and quick
cremation.

✳ 3.

do not wait to be loved
seek it,
the unexplainable.
fight for love
not knowing whether you have
lost or accomplished
poetic possibilities.
dig deep for love
search while acknowledging
the complexity of the heart & fading standards.
in seeking love use care.
to let strangers come into you
too quickly
may make you a stranger to yourself.

4.

from dawn to dusk in cities
that sunrises often fail to visit

we imprisoned light
& generated heat.

you are seedless grapes and
bright stars at winter & wind.
there are voices in your smiles
and confirmation in the parting of your lips.

you speak in laughter and pain,
are vibrant youth approaching dreams
knowing disappointment,
accepting quality.

The Changing Seasons of Ife

she is quality and light
a face of carob and ivory
of broad smiles and eyes that work.
she dresses in purples
& touches of aquablue.
plants grow profusely in her earthpots.
she seeks standards,
will not accept questionable roses or tapped water.
her taste is antique and bountiful heritage,
her music often void of melody
is firetone and harsh truths.
it is known that
dark rhythms played in & out of her early years
leaving temporary scars that lined her future
as beauty has it
wine is shared with shadows on prolonged trips
her smile broad & brandy
makes small miracles
emerge.

Lady Day

hearing from you are smiles in winter
you   as you are
you warm and illuminating spaces
bring
blooming fruit in iceage times
with heated heated voices

believe me when i say
men will listen to you
most
will try to please you

there will be sun & thunder & mudslides
in your life
you will satisfy your days with work & laughter
and sunday songs.
your nights like most nights will
conjure up memories of easier seasons
happier suntimes and coming years

earthcolors and rainbows will enter your heart
when least expected
often
in small enduring ways   like this
lovesong.

Some of the Women are Brave

her strength may have come from
not having the good things early in life
like
her own bed, unused clothes,
"good looks", uncritical friends
or
from the knee of her great grandmother.
whatever path she took
she was learning to become small danger.

organizer of mothers
overseer of broken contracts,
a doer of large deeds,
unafraid of sky scrapers & monotone
bureaucrats.
monotones labeled her demands crippling & unusual.
she urged drinkable water, working elevators,
clean playgrounds, heat, garbage collection
and the consolation of tenant's dreams.

many dammed her,
others thought her professional agitator & provocateur
dismissing her as a
man hating bull digger
that was communist inspired.

she was quick burn against the enemy
a stand up boxer unattached to niceties
and the place of women.
she was waterfalls in the brain
her potency as it comes
needs to be packaged & overnight expressed
to Black homes; to be
served with morning meals.

Search Void of Fear

bronzed fire among the cold of cold,
she was happy moments & clear fields.
she was touch & yellow
softrose with eyes that begged of sleep,
eyes that penetrated the cold of cold.

g.c. was lover & giver
searcher void of fear.
distances would be her metaphor
from cleveland to afrika over ocean & desert
travel expressed the search in her,
highlighting the afrikan in her.

just around her 28th season
g.c. passed through devastating hurt,
resulting in early burial of her man.
this is not talked of. her ancestors
demanded that she not be imprisoned with
dead thoughts or warm memories.

she was destined to be
searcher void of fear and
cold seconds should not detour
a softrose with eyes that begged of sleep.
often
she was happy moments & clear fields,
she was sun ripped and ready for war
indeed
ready for love.

Womenblack: We begin with You
(for Safisha)

our women we begin with you
black, beige, brown, yellowblack and
darkearth we dropped from your womb
in joyscreams lifegiver
you're worlds apart from the rest.

our women
imagine a warm breeze in any city
in the west that will not choke you,
be wife, be mother, a worker or professional
maker you still my lady.
our women
of fruits & vegetables
of greens & color   of sounds & pot holes
of mountains & earth clearing danger   from
doorways who did not ruin their teeth & bodies
with the blood of pigs & cattle or fried chicken
after stumppin at bob's place til five in the daylight.
partyin was almost like a job
in motion on the run we are the rhythm people.

womenblack
unusual maker you say,
fine as all getout you say,
finer than lemonade in the shade,
we are a part of you maker, woman of
the autumn earth mother of sunlight
& i seldom say "i love you"
love is not our word. love belongs to
soap operas & comic books, is the true
confessions of the pale people from
the winter's cold.
we are the people of motion, move on motion
dance on, summer, summer lady.

womenblack we care about you
a deep & uncontrollable penetrative
care   as we listen to our own hearts,
whatever the weather.
you don't have to build a pyramid
in order to be one & you are still my
maker rhythm, rhythm lady.

our women we begin with you
black, beige, brown, yellowblack and
darkearth we dropped from your womb
in joyscreams lifegiver
you're worlds apart from the best.
you are in me & i in you
deep
deep and endless
forever
touch to touch,
end to beginning
until the stars kiss the earth
and
our music will be songs of liberation.

Struggle

some called her
sunshine others berryblack
she was woman twice
layed way way back
her smile was winning wide
her teeth glowed and captured light
she was woman twice
men thought her mighty nice

deep black off brown and mississippi grown lula mae
was careful. she had experienced the heartaches,
heard the stories and often hid the tears. lula mae
was more watcher and listener now. yes, her emotions
were still there, real & womanly strong but they had
failed her too often in the past, her lovers had left
memories that distorted her forehead and scars that
even she didn't want to acknowledge.

(pretty willie g left his fist print under her left ear,
larry the pimp provided her with a dislocated hip and
baby frank left her in $3000 debt and promises of
short life is she mentioned his whereabouts.)

lula mae now sought other signs of caring. she
wanted relationships that were not so one sided, short
termed or physically risky. she looked for verbal
confirmation, evening phone calls, unexpected love
notes and deep back and foot massages at the day's
end. lula mae not yet 30 knew that she was special,
knew that her capacity for love was unusual and also
knew that the next man in her life would understand
and appreciate this specialness before he got any of
it.

what will it be?
when will Blackmen learn that
fist & feet against the teeth
is like removing the heart of a people.
who will teach us
that slaps & kicks & verbal lashings
detour sharing, stops bonding
destroy unifiers, retard respect & eliminate
connecting vision.
what will it be?
what messenger, what unmutted voice
will clarify touching
detail body contact without blackeyes?
what caller will articulate
disagreements without boxing,
love
without force.
where are the bold & rejuvenated men
and women that will head this most needed of
revolutionary struggles?

A Mother's Poem
(for G.B.)

not often do we talk.
destruction was to be mine at 28
a bullet in the head   or
wrong handed lies that would lock
me in pale cells that are designed to
cut breathing and Will.
you gave me maturity at daybreak
slashed my heart
and slowed the sprint toward extinction,
delayed my taking on the world alone,
you made living a laborious & loving commitment.

you shared new blood,
challenged mistaken vision,
suggested frequent smiles,
while enlarging life to more than
daily confrontations and lost battles
fought by unprepared poets.

not often did we talk.
your large acts of kindness shaped memory,
your caring penetrated bone & blood
and permanently sculptured a descendant.
i speak of you in smiles
and seldom miss a moment
to thank you for
saving a son.

RAINFOREST

you are forest   rain
dense with life green colors
forever pulling the blue of life into you
see you walk and
i would like to burst rainwater into you
swim in & out of you
opening you like anxious earthquakes
uncontrollable but beautiful & dangerous.

get with this woman   come
fire frozen beauty,
men cannot sleep around you
your presence demands attention
demands notice
demands touch & motion & communication.

you are runner
swift like warm wind hurricanes
fast like stolen firebirds
& you disrupt the silence in me
make me speak memories long forgotten & unshared.
secrets uttered in strange storms,
deep full sounds reserved for magical,
magical lovers.

listen runner
i have shared pain with you,
i have commented on future worlds to you,
i have let you touch the weak & strong of me,
i have tasted the tip of your ripeness &
kissed sweat from your middle.
i have bit into your mouth &

sucked the lifeforces from yr insides   and
i know you. understand you.
i have shared books & travel & music & growth with you.

sweet knows honey & i know you.
under salted water tides
& running against polluted earth
i've tried to be good to you woman
tried to care beyond words
          care beyond distant spaces
sensitive phases & quiet lies
care
beyond cruel music & false images.

you are original high & dream maker
& true men do not try to limit you.

listen woman black
i do not wish to dominate your dreams
or obstruct your vision.
trust my motion   feel
know that i am near and with you
& will cut the cold of winter winds to reach you.
you
are delicate bronze
in spring-summers and special autumns
you are forest   rain
dark & runner & hurricane-black
frequently
i say frequently i bring you
midnight   **rain**.

the New men Black
are tongue silent,
hawkeyed and
dangerous
many who should
know say
that these men
do not play
or
pass blank checks
the word is that
these men
cannot be
bought.

THE MEN

In The Gut or Give Me Five: An Introduction

How many of you without doubt or hesitation can point out five Black men, locally or nationally, whose first priority is the liberation of Black people? How many of you can name five Black men right now, from the top of your head, who you believe under any circumstances, would not betray or sell out Black people for personal or political gain? Can you identify five true Black leaders who have not been compromised by money, white women, white privileged, oversized egos and media fame? Herein lies the legacy of our hurt. Serious and unbought Black men are few and fewer.

The century is not over. Let me issue this warning. Music comes in strange tones. The notes of our melodies are fast, slow and complexingly rhythmic. The songs of struggle must be unpredictable. The music players must constantly practice and continuously train body and mind. To become accomplished music makers there is but one method for serious preparation: study, train, practice, strive to tone the physical with the mental and the spiritual so that they function as one. Be reliable and proactive.

Study your strengths and weaknesses. Know your body like sweet knows honey. Keep yourself lean, hard and ready for war. Deeply examine the way of life. We must erase the landscapes of fear and inaction. Atlanta and Buffalo are still with us. Black life in America is cheap and according to the world runners, highly dispensable. Hear me well. There are white men (and women) in this country (and the world) who see as their God given task, the effective neutralization of the Black movement, which at its base means the systematic destruction of Black boys and men. Violent aggression against Black men is nothing new; however, what is most revealing is that the current aggression against Blacks is taking place after two decades of "so-called" Black advancement. Only the critically weak-minded can fail to see the picture on the screen.

Active, consistent and effective Black struggle is our only **oasis.** As we travel the desert of our time, take a few minutes during the day to listen to the heartbeat of our children, stop often and look into their eyes, survey their smiles (if they are there) and ask yourself this question: **Do I want my children to be crippled zombies, incapable of decision or movement, totally dependent on the chief criminals of the world for their survival and development?** If the answer is **yes**, simply go back to sleep. If your answer is **NO** quietly yet quickly start to transform your life. Critically assess the Word (study), don't give quarter or comfort to the enemy, learn to hide tears and anger with smiles and planning. Above all, believe, in the gut, that we can — Black men and women-create a better, better world.

learn from those who die early
mistakes are hidden lessons
learn from those who are killed doing good
they recognized
however late
the business we all should be about.

The Destruction of Fathers

at the beginning he felt that it gave him
                                        time
to do the acts of importance that somehow
he was unable to do   before
the vacating of rooms   before
the clearing of book shelves & dresser drawers
before the
greed of lawyers
tears of children   and
draining sleeplessness of fathers.

divorce generated an abundance of
                                    time
to hear,
to contemplate the missing the mistakes
                                        time
to seek pure noise,
for self inflicted wounds,
planned interruptions,
& suicidal waiting moments   for
wishing & rushing of weekend visits

at thirty-eight it was a devastating   time
to have lost wife, children and familiar spaces
to "irreconcilable differences",
obsolete definitions & rapid firing mouth.

again
it was a devastating   time with only
quiet to debate at whether men should
share in garbage emptying, floor mopping,
dish washing, laundry doing, shopping, &c.
when one is alone there are no questions
only time
and clarity arriving
too late.

Poet: for Larry Neal

in time and time
in evening nights
in quiet search and final answer
they took the poets away

they promised them gifts of gifts and portable and
    lasting fame
they promised them beautiful life, hungerless days,
    rising riches
and lasting lust. they promised gold & university chairs
    & unlimited
publication.

they promised promises
and
in return
they suggested that the poets
sing a
falsesong.

this world is full of
missing,
and dying
& unpublished
poets.

My Brothers

my brothers i will not tell you
who to love or not love
i will only say to you
that
Black women have not been
loved enough.

i will say to you
that
we are at war & that
Black men in america are
being removed from the
earth
like loose sand in a wind storm
and that the women Black are
three to each of us.

no
my brothers i will not tell you
who to love or not love
but
i will make you aware of our
self hating and hurting ways.
make you aware of whose bellies
you dropped from.
i will glue your ears to those images
you reflect which are not being
loved.

The Damage We Do

he loved his women
weak & small
so that he would not tire
of
beating them.
he sought the weakest & the smallest
so that they couldn't challenge
his rage of boxing
their heads up against refrigerators,
slamming their hands in doors,
stepping on them like roaches,
kicking them in their centers of life.
all of his women
were
weak and small and sick
& he an
embarrassment to the human form
was not an exception in america.

Rape: the male crime

there are mobs & strangers
in us
who scream of the women
wanted and
will get
as if the women are ours for the
taking.

our mothers, sisters, wives and
daughters ceased to be the
women men want   we think of them as
loving family   music & soul   bright wondermints.
they are not locker room talk
not the hunted lust or   dirty
cunt burnin hoes.
bright wondermints are excluded   by association as
blood & heart   bone & memory
& we will destroy a rapist's knee caps,
& write early grave on his thoughts
to protect them.

it will do us large to recall
when the animal in us rises
that all women are someone's
mother, sister, wife or daughter
and are not fruit to be stolen when hungry.

a significant few of their
fathers, brothers, husbands, sons
and growing strangers
are willing to unleash harm on the earth
and spill blood in the eyes
of

maggots in running shoes
who do not know the sounds of birth
or respect the privacy of the human form.

 **White on Black Crime**

lately and not by choice
milton washington is self employed.
workin hard
he collects aluminum cans,
pop bottles, papers & cardboard
and sells them to the
local recycling center.

milton washington is an unemployed
master welder who has constantly sought
work in & out of his trade.
he is now seen on beaches, in parks,
in garbage cans, leaving well lit allies
in the evenings pushing one cart
& pulling the other, head to the side
eyes glued southward long steppin homeward.

milton's unemployment ran out 14 months ago.
first the car went & he questioned his manhood.
next the medical insurance, savings & family
nights out ceased & he questioned his god.
finally his home was snatched & he disappeared
for two days & questioned his dreams
and all he believed in.

milton works a 15 hour day &
recently redefined his life for
the sixth time selecting as his only goal
the housing, feeding & keeping his family
together.

yesterday the payout per pound
on aluminum was reduced by 1/4 cent

as the stock market hit an all time high
& the president smiled through a speech
on economic recovery, welfare cheats & the
availability of jobs for those who want to work.

milton washington has suffered
the humiliation of being denied food stamps,
the laughter and cat calls of children,
the misunderstanding in the eyes of his family
and friends.
milton belived in the american way
even hung flags on the fourth & special days
and demanded the respect of god & country in
his home.

at 1/4 cent reduction in pay per pound
milton washington will have to add
an hour and a half to his 15 hour day.
milton washington, more american than black,
quiet and resourceful, a collector of dreams
cannot close his eyes anymore,
cannot excuse the failure in his heart,
cannot expect miracles in daylight,
is real close, very, very close to hurtin somebody
real bad.

A Poem for Quincy Jones, Sidney Poitier, Harry Belafonte, Kareem Abdul Jabar, James Earl Jones, Wilt Chamberlain, Richard Pryor, Redd Foxx, Lou Rawls, &c., &c., &c. for Days

it is actual and prophetic   that
when the money comes
when the fame and autograph seekers arrive,
when there is something to share & wear,
that the **root** is forced into basements,
backrooms and aching embarrassment.

acts toward the indigenous become frigid cliches
(after children wrecking & torturous, rise to the
          penacle)
the **root** is now tolerated baggage & excessive worry,
a for real style cramper & potential court warrior.
for him the current revelation is that
"people are just people"
converting the universe into one gigantic lovefest.
exempting
the berrycolored   nappyheaded   rustykneed
exempting
the widehipped   biglipped   cherrybrown women.

his eyes have gone pink sucking
venom from the people
who less than a word ago
less than a few missed meals ago
used his ass as a shoe shiner.
          tap tap dance do the bounce now
          do the white boy richard 357 magnum yr car
          shoot death in yr toe freebase raw brilliance
          fire up tap tap tap dance run out da pain in da
          brain.

stardom is the ultimate drug,

fame fogs tradition   dismembers values
& elevates egos to cocaine highs.
idol status
is volcanic to the insides   evaporates memory
& neutralizes kindness.
the **root**
the unbought memory of the culture
flows red in the women
when the women are traded and reduced to
matrilineal burning bitches
bleeding sets in   families decay
rendering generational destruction
producing final stop orders.

ask your momma.

 **Comin Strong**

And where are the men Black and ready?
some say,
they've lost their way
beneath pig's litter & fool's gold.
others say,
they are hid under political deception
& three dollar bills returning in numbers
as colored traitors clothed in abundance.

the real word is that the men have become
pregnant with spoiled food
& thoughts of false grandeur.
they drive boat cars,
smoke strange weeds,
destroy their noses with crippling dust,
manicure their nails
& talk wrong about their women.
some say,
it is best that these men stay lost.

the new men Black
do not measure themselves in
the way of the elusive streets
do not look toward the west as the test.
the new men Black with dust & dirt
are clear thinkers and city learned
are not tied to garbage cans & whiskey breath.
these men take their sons seriously &
listen closely to their daughters.
they do not come as beggars or buyers
they are teachers and doers returning in
a force that's unimaginable.

the new men Black are
tongue silent, hawkeyed and dangerous.
many who should know say
that these men do not play,
do not pass blank checks.
they say that these men cannot be
bought.

Black Manhood: Toward a Definition

your people first. a quiet strength. the positioning of
oneself so that observation comes before reaction,
where study is preferred to night life, where emotion
is not seen as a weakness. love for self, family,
children, and extentions of self is beyond the verbal.

Black manhood. making your life accessible to children in meaningful ways. able to recognize the war
we are in & doing anything to take care of family
so long as it doesn't harm or negatively affect other
Black people. willing to share resources to the
maximum, willing to struggle unrelentingly against
the evils of this world especially evils that directly
threaten the development of our people.

Black manhood. to seek and be that which is just,
good and correct. properly positioning oneself in the
context of our people. a listener, a student, a
historian seeking hidden truths. one who develops
leadership qualities and demands the same qualities
of those who have been chosen to lead. see material
rewards as means toward an end & not an end in
themselves. clean-mentally, spiritually & physically.
protector of Black weak. one who respects elders.
practical idealist, questioner of the universe &
spiritually in tune with the best of the universe.
honest & trusting, your word is your connector.

Black manhood. direction giver. husband. sensitive to
Black women's needs and aspirations, realizing that it
is not necessary for them to completely absorb
themselves into us but that nothing separates the
communication between us. a seeker of truth. a
worker of the first order. teacher. example of what

is to be. fighter. a builder with vision. connects land
to liberation. a student of peace & war. statesman
and warrior. one who is able to provide as well as
receive. culturally sound. creative. a motivator &
stimulator of others.

Black manhood. a lover of life and all that is
beautiful. one who is constantly growing and who
learns from mistakes. a challenger of the known and
the unknown. the first to admit that he does not
know as he seeks to find out. able to solicit the
best out of self and others. soft. strong. not afraid
to take the lead. creative father. organized and
organizer. a brother to brothers. a brother to sisters.
understanding. patient. a winner. maintainer of the i
can, i must, i will attitude toward Black struggle
& life. a builder of the necessary. **always** & always in
a process of growth and without a doubt believes that
our values and traditions are not negotiable.

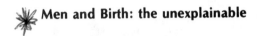# Men and Birth: the unexplainable

malepractice & maleabsence issue is loneliness & limiting tomorrows. men need to experience rising screams. husbands, lovers, fathers, menfriends should be with their wives, women before. during & after. helping them weather labor and lonely storms. we, locating new climates & seasons working with midwives, doctors & wife allowing them to take you back to school. you, who thought that baby delivering was others work, stranger's work.

welcome to new seasons of wisdom.
welcome to counting & breathing,
to pushing & contractions,
to urging life onward quietly &
magnificently.

muffled grunts interrupt sleep urging participation counting push pushing encouraging your mate to relax to breath properly, constantly setting the mental clock. in the bed at her rear pulling legs back enlarging womb creating unbelievable spaces wider urging life here. men viewing & aiding the unquestioned miracle on earth. sliding head first helpless struggling searching attacking life into waiting hands baby crying for mother & loving touches. this is the drama, **birth** the maturing force that can transform males. making them men of conscious. making them bringers of life and partners in the fight to guarantee better better futures.

birth
unlocks cultural strangulation allowing
men to feel & touch & experience
a source of love that spring in
smiles occasional tears and   undying commitment.

Message to Our Sons ✳

son,
do not forget the women killed
by the whites & men negro made white.
do not disregard the women Black
killed for closing their legs to
bodies foreign to their insides,
for preserving the culture of their foreparents,
for daring to be the just.
son, let your memory not erase
or betray the sacred teachings of
these women. mothers, sisters, lovers and wives
whom the world has transgressed against.
record their tracks in code and memory.
my son do not neglect our women nor
forgive those who have **violated**
a precious part of you.

For Blackmen with Integrity and Convictions

there are people beyond clout and distance
who have orders
from above   on high   to do you
debilitating harm
worse than broken knee caps and twisted face
worse than ruining your good name or destroying your
    marriage
worse than turning your friends and people against
    you.

they have final stop orders
these people have cleaned weapons,
sharpened skills,
have mapped your every movement,
booked your weaknesses & dissected your strengths
you are a considerable foe
& many are preparing to exterminate you with
"extreme prejudice"

their design
is to close the history books on your name,
crown you traitor & child molestor.
anything
to erase the people's positive memory of you.

it will be difficult to brace
against this storm.

continue as you must
intensify and insulate
let them know that
they're in for a fight.

Take hold,
do the
Necessary,
reverse,
destruction
capture
tomorrows.

DESTINY

✳Get Fired Up

get fired up
get excited about hue and dark colors
ignite truth in the temple
there will be many who will try to take you out
watch the light shadows
exemplify & scream cleanliness into the world
leave yr mark
the children must know that you
& you   & you
carried the message.

Hanging Hard in America

one does not want to hurt   the word is th'at
bodies break easily in the west   the word is that
the important articles are made of plastic & glue
put together by people whose major aim is
profit:
  made in japan is no longer laughable
  enter hong kong, taiwan, singapore, &c.,
  to buy american is not quality its patriotic,
  the way is buy now pay if you catch me,
  get it now tomorrow may be never,
  pay for what you want beg for the needs.

families are disappearing.
children & vegetation are back seated
& automobiles and canned foods are the
measurements of normality. family bonding
or preparing for the long hike is what the crazy do.
lips thunder everywhere talking in tongues praising
"my god" & intellectual pursuits like reading & thinking
are left to fools, bureaucrats, compromising scholars
& a few starving & unlettered poets.

the urgent quests are for new money markets,
i. magnum & neiman marcus accounts.
it is taught that light shines on those who can
afford electricity & new definitions depend on your
politics and cash flow:
right means don't do it,
integrity translates as square,
honesty is lonely,
the rich are correct,
the poor are lazy,
loyalty is rewards in suitcases after dark &

the world is never too small for liars,
only for amateurs. were you not told that
professionals do not fabricate the truth they become
historians and anthropologists & reinterpret reality.

so we hurt,
we learn to hate as we dig in
for the long track.
as should be our ancestors speak wisdom:
do not send your children to be taught by
those who do not love them;
raise strong, loving and sane children and
we will not have to repair broken adults.
above all the final call is:
do not forgive violation of people & loss of language,
do not forget dirt in the eye & the middle passage.

America: the future

in a country

where pride is measured
in body counts

a black
school aged boy
pledged
allegiance to the flag

as the words came
he
thought about today's
ball game
& about the
homeruns he would hit
& his special willie mays catch

he didn't remember the flag
until after
he noticed the
cancelled sign on the ball park's gate

that night he asked
his momma:
        "momma why the flag got holes in it?"
her reply:
        "daddy's back."

We Struggle for The Children
   (for Lu Palmer & the independent school
   movement)

in between nights party strong,
in between mortgages & debt ridden promises,
in between eyes blued to the tube **dude**
look for the children.
   **in between pimps and hoes slammin cadillac
   dooes, in between mad & sane, gone & where,
   locate the next generation.**
spend as much time with yr offspring
as you do picking yr wardrobe freddy be
check their blank faces & unknown futures,
check their fading smiles & bodies weakening under
lies, neglect & the ruin of the west.
look for the children **clean**
as you out dress the best in the west.

check yr image trackman
it is a fact, a sure bet
that you know mo bout them horses
than yr own son two dollar willie?
observe the young big mac, swinging sue & set down
   eddy,
give attention to the coming adults
dr. morris, rev. jones, atty. wills, judge christian
as you negotiate for yr new ride,
as you prepare for yr next trip to the islands,
as you manicure yr nails & press yo head.
look toward tomorrow dancing billy & ms. clairol
as you take that next drink,
as you construct that dynamite joint & make ready
to bump all weekend in yr customized van.
what of the dependents many locked in other worlds?
   **in between pimps & hoes slammin cadillac
   dooes, in between mad & sane, gone & where**

here & how
locate the next generation.

check their faces Black with vision,
in between summer homes & confused purposes,
 in between gangster walls & sun roofs,
in between hated gigs & long weekends,
in between one piece suits & wall to wall lip,
in between hit & miss, get & get it,
think about something beautiful, blood.

Black children growing into brightness,
smile to smile in between the in betweens,
wind against wind binding toward the good,
be what is necessary **momma,**
claim this mountain **baba,**
give 30 minutes a day to yr children's development,
give books & trips,
encouragement and growing examples,
supply the enriching needs teachers.

be what you want your children to be.
practice and extend the family,
live and love Blacklife,
always and always until ignorance is vanquished
and our smiles are not
painful disguises for failure.

Art: A comment
(for Murry, Calvin, Jeff, Bing, Helen, Jon, Akili,
Roy, Bob, Freida & the NCA)

the summer & winter beauty
of a people's culture rides
heroicly in their arts.
study human creation for the secrets to
killers & saints,
fools & wise speakers.
search their music for heartbeat,
    their drama for recall and tomorrows,
    their literature for Will and vision,
    their visualforms for uncluttered love and moun-
        tains.
the art makers
those tenacious forgers of truth
are hungry for your smile,
they know in america that plastic & soaps are in,
that the cry is sameness in the skyscrapers and
the captive form is to defeat flowers
& strap concrete to ideas
while pursuing relationships that would
embarrass babies.
among the new & few
it is accepted that art exposes
rats in the crib,
clowns in the temple,
idiots in the congress,
rot in the wheat.
**art provides the beat the tellin heat the ellington
    bounce**
**wright's anger brooks' hook dunham's glide the
    feelings' feel & field.**
the rounded callin cards
washing change in the city,
    fightin suffocation & money looking for investments

110

are
visionaries claiming elegant & ugly.
artist
do not seek immortality
seek ears & eyes   minds & conformation
seek smiles in the young   change in the motion
& beware of harm in the daylight and of nations
planning cross cultural trips to afrika
while simultaneously implanting your image on
postage stamps.

BIKO

water dripping   drop by drop
into the ears of the broederbond*
leaving them water logged and senseless
desperately appreciating pain.
knowing the displacement of dreams
knowing what slavery is and raw smiles of Black
    mommas
following husbands to shanty towns to squat in
    squalor & mud is.

to be born among apologists
in a land taken from one's ancestors
is a profound comment on how far
we have lost our way.

to be born among weaker apologies
from color men in white collars
who constantly preach "a better day a comin,"
tomorrow

expect tennis and cricket,
jogging, handball & polo played on manicured greens.
better days of beer and evening playgrounds
and admission to divinity schools.
but never   never
the retrieval of one's land.

as the young   young men & women
steal away into the heat of the heart
seeking the uncompromising past in search of
clear sight inciting the alerting question,
"why did they kill Steve Biko?"
their message to Black america,
"don't send us no ribbins to wear."

* The white brotherhood that controls power in South Afrika.

Sun and Storm

beyond weep and whisper,
beyond clown and show,
beyond why & where & not now
clear the voices

there is **storm** on the horizon.
beneath calm & cold & killer death
there is **vision** approaching.
beneath filth & fear & running asses
there is planning & hope & connecting trust.
beneath traffic stops and sex crazed negroes
there are new people arising
clothed in love & work & a will to advance.

newpeople
bold and sure   tested tough   fever wise
these are womenblack with brain and womb &
smiles that regenerate.
these are menblack with mind and seed &
strength of strength.
they are children conscious and elder wise
sweet lovers of life.
newpeople
known in afrika,
known in asia,
known in europe & the americas
with their rainbow smiles, willing minds,
and bridge building backs as the
people of the sun.

End Notes

if parting is necessary
part as lovers.
part as two people
who can still
smile & talk & share
the good & important
with each other.
part
wishing the other
happy
happy life
in a world
fighting against the
beautiful,
fighting against the
men & women,
sisters and brothers
Black as
we.

Future

first
it is between the black and the black
come
not as empty earth,
not as wasted energy,
not as apologetic color consciousness,
not as fool blinded to light,
not as imitation cardboard.

come
as gifted lovers
eyes bright & daring life.
come
as ripening fruit
quick smiles and joyous words.
come
woman to man
man to woman
pursuing the way of life
within the colors of vision
between the
black and the black.

Earthquakes

(for Frances Cress Welsing)

in the hot of the eye
at the insertion of cayanne
what really matters is:
children catching breath,
children experiencing love and continuation,
children understanding the good and emerging evil,
children expecting a future,
children smiling quickly and uninhibited
in this world.
        as the smiles cease conflict beckons
        hearts hurt   blood rushes   hands sweat
        pain ensues and comes like pins in the spine
understand this:
conscious men do not make excuses
do not expect their women to carry their water,
harvest the food and prepare it too.
world over it is known that
breast sucking is only guaranteed to babies.
    ✹ sisters if the men do not fight,
        if the men are not responsible
cover the breast   close the legs   stop the love
cancel good times   erase privileges   question man-
    hood.

if the men engage the enemy
get ready for rumor & devisive headaches
everyone will want to know their price,
traitors will try & confirm that the men can be
    bought,
enemies will pass gold to family & lovers to buy his
    dreams.
if the engaged men are of the wise kind
they will appreciate the greater needs and
without doubt or hesitation tell them our pay back is:

georgia, the states of florida & alabama, we want
texas.

when the smiles quit when the laughter quiets
conflict beckons   hearts hurt   blood rushes
     hands sweat
spine strengthens   & brothers comprehend.
catch the sun & get on up
rise on the run. open eyed
ready & expecting danger

expecting earthquakes.

Sun Rise Missions: (for Hoyt W. Fuller)

He will be missed, not lost among papers
remembered in midnight study cells
and early morning runs.
remembered as an originator of
wisdom
from a vision that was sound & sane
steadfast and tempered
Tempo between songs and dance   between
fist and articulation   call him
screamingly dangerous

Sang beauty first
notice the eyes of children
locate their living & eating space
try & smile now.
run with & against the common wind
do damage for damage be
unpredictable with map and compass
& weapons pressed against the cheek

Catch fire & fire
notice
there is an uneasiness among us
window shades are drawn,
people talk in nods and whispers
babies are again born in homes,
people are picking up books and nails
and anxiously listening to grandparents.
there is sunrise on the horizon
Pass this word quickly and quietly
there are rats in the streets.

Poison is needed. Now.

Destiny

under volcanoes & timeless years within watch
and low tones. around corners, in deep caves among
misunderstood and sometimes meaningless sounds.
cut beggars, outlaw pimps & whores. resurrect work.
check your distance blue
come
earthrise men deepblack and ready
come
sunbaked women rootculture on the move.

just do what you're suppose to do
just do what you say you gonta do
not the impossible,
not the unimaginative,
not copy clothed as original and surely
not bitter songs in european melodies.

take hold
do the necessary, the possible, the correctly simple
take hold
talk of missions & interpret destiny
put land and selfhood on the minds of our people
do the expected,
do what all people do

reverse destruction.
capture tomorrows.

Remembering
the
Middle Passage:
Culture as Motion

**Why Life in America is Not Working For Black People
And What Needs To Be Done To Change The Future**

I

A people's view of themselves as well as the
world has to be a long one if they are to be more
than a footnote in history. To reconstruct memory is
to invoke possibilities and accent permanence. How
do a people forget? What are the conditions that
erase cultures? What is it in the makeup of a people
that allow them to belittle their own traditions and
make small of themselves and their history? Why do a
people forget? Understand that I am not talking about
individual loss of memory, but that of an entire
people (exempting, possibly, the blessed few who
somehow continue to wage the quiet fight for
substance and renewal). The comprehensive answer to
my questions are undoubtedly lost with the countless
mothers who chose abortion and death rather than
suffer the intrusion of foreign bodies and rootlessness;
lost with Afrikan men beaten and shaken beyond
comprehension, deciding to smile at death rather than
endure the humiliation of enslavement and the

ultimate defeat of the spirit through the subjugation and misuse of their women and children. The Middle Passage was the key, turning the memory lock. The ocean was a destroyer, a supreme separator of body from soil, spirit from soul, mind from source.

What I am questioning is, can you imagine pain? Pain greater than limbs severed in an automobile accident; pain not unlike nails driven into the heart. What happens to the mind that in one second is in complete command of one's own destiny; free to work, build, play, love and make use of one's creative juices; and in less than a blinking eye one is reduced to a number on a sea captain's ledger, redefined out of the human family, diminished to a state of personal property to be bartered or sold worldwide as a **slave?** The long road to amnesia begins when a man is forced to view the rape of his women; the dismantling of his family and nation; the forceful sprinkling of his children worldwide and the occupation of his land by foreigners unlike any people he has known. How does a woman survive the castration of her men; the loss of her insides and detachment from all that was beautiful and meaningful to her without mental dislocation? What happends to the mind that experiences family dismantlement and the distribution of its members into the services of another race for life? The choices, after defeat, were limited and what confirmed the limitations was when one was forced into the holes of ships, in spaces that crippled the body, and then transported thousands of miles under incredible conditions that were designed to destroy the spirit with each mile traveled from the land of one's beginning. The crowning blow was to be unloaded in strange ports among even stranger people and systematically traumatized into a different and ugly way of life.

In order to survive, one had to give up

something, and if that something was not the body, the only explainable substitute was the mind; it goes, snaps like steel under intense heat; the mind, once fire and light, snaps under the force of ocean and darkness seeking peace in forgetfulness. The mind, that magnificent force that separates human from animal, genius from idiot; now a confused mass cluttered with defeat, betrayal, shame and loneliness. For many people death would have been a reward, but for the Afrikan, reward was to be made anew in Europe and beyond.

Reconstruction of the Afrikan self was to be just about impossible. Slowly, but effectively, those moments that secured and identified one with one's people began to fade; the names became un-Afrikan; new Gods were adopted; the climate dictated different clothing; history became recent and that of appreciated victims; the deathblow that signaled undeniable defeat occurred quite by surprise; no one, not even the elders, could speak the language of their foreparents. With the killing of the language, the transfiguration of the Afrikans was complete and lasting. Yet, there remain important elements of Afrikan culture to which the people hold tight such as Afrikan humanism, a deep spirituality, etc; however, few things are as important as language and for most, the quieting of the tongue, more than anything else, sealed their faith in the new world, for without language one cannot express the indigenous self, and therefore, one has nothing to express other than the selves of others in their language.

II

Most people in the world are economically poor. Much of the world's people are directly or indirectly still tied to the land, thus receiving most of their income from the land via agriculture. The economic gains that most of the world's people earn for their day's labor is not enough to feed, clothe, house or educate them. I add education to the three basic needs because I feel that education or enlightment is an absolute need just as the others are because if provided in a progressive manner, it can loosen the chains of the land. In this age of scientific and technological development, it is indeed backward and somewhat debilitating for a family to have to work from sun up to sun down six to seven days a week just to earn the bare necessities of life.

What is most disturbing is to see that the people who, for the most part, are in this predicament are people of color who have been redefined as "third world people" and out of their number, close to one billion of them are Blacks. In the United States this Black poor is not so much tied to the land*, but has become the new urban Black underclass that is totally dependent upon the state for its existence. This Black urban poor is not only landless but has little, if any of the "so called" new wealth that has been produced by the United States' current service orientated and information gathering economy. This urban Black poor in the United States is landless, penniless, politically unsophisticated and defenseless. A position that some commentators described as the New Scientific Slavery. That Europe and the majority of the western world enjoy the highest standard of living in the world

---

* As of 1981, Black farmers and landowners have lost eleven million acres. According to the Emergency Land Fund of Atlanta, Georgia, Blacks loose 9,615 acres of land per week (500,000 acres annually) and by 1984 if this trend continues, Black people will be landless in the U.S.

for the least people hours worked is not mystical nor does it have anything to do with the stars. Economic struggle is natural, most people worldover try to better their economic conditions. Men and women, since the beginning of recorded history, have struggled against nature and its forces. To the degree that people have been able to control, divert, insulate, work with and harvest natural resources, speaks directly to that people's development or non-development. The fight to move beyond day to day existence took centuries to perfect. Economic as well as political struggle, is on going and over the last five hundred years has taken a more dangerous focus subordinating the fight against nature to that of the fight between humans and humans, nations against nations, race against race, cultures against cultures for the leadership and resources of the woprld. The Struggle between nations is now a world concern because for the first time in human history several nations, all white, have the ability to destroy all forms of life on earthwith the possible exception of the ever present roach.

My focus here is not necessarily a history lesson. I am not a historian, a student of history yes, but not one who has exclusively devoted his very life to its understanding. What has fascinated me is why it is that when given the same variables - knowledge base, land, intellectual inquisitiveness, climate, etc. - that one people move progressively forward and another people, under similar conditions, barely survive? I am convinced that originally the reason had little to do with genetics (biology) or race but dealt more with the ability of a people, any people, to plan and execute their worldview, to evaluate historical trends and learn from them; to make mistakes and not be destroyed as a result of

125

them to accept constructive criticism and act on it while at the same time working to use in their best interest the land, climate and other geological forces. Also a wise and determined people will develop a mythology (sacred and secular) that will bind them together against internal and external enemies. They will create a workable and developmental **positive information bank** that is "equally" accessible to the majority. A wise people will maintain and create a leadership network that is not exclusively confined or regulated to one economic, political or religious sector. An enlightened people will encourage and maintain an ongoing research and development sector for domestic as well as international affairs, create a highly professional armed forces that is dedicated to the highest ideals of that people, and finally, a developed people will have a human service sector that will encourage in the people the preventive health aspects of life while allowing the existence of an economy that has an "equal" potential for upward mobility, that is, a humane society will function best for the majority and will not necessarily have many gigantic economic gaps among its people but will encourage collective as well as individual economic development.

It is clear, if we care to take off the blinders, that the West, in terms of basic scientific, techno-logical and economical "development", is light years ahead of much of the world. Another way of stating this is that the West is enjoying its time in history and is taking advantage of all opportunities. Other than it being one's time in history, why is the West in such a dominating position on the world stage? The answer is not a simple one and cannot be reduced to slogans or one word answers such as colonialism, monopoly capitalism, or racism but for brevity can be con-densed to two factors: 1) The Western—European and

USA view of the world has gone beyond the previously cherished views. The knowns and unknowns that generally handicapped a people's development, mainly religious restraint, ceased to exist about 500 years ago as Europe challenged and questioned all aspects of life including the existence of a **God.** Therefore, in most "advanced" European nations—Germany, France, England—there was the development of two lines of thought—the sacred (religious) and the secular (scientific), both steeped in white supremacist ideology. These two different and often opposing theories were in conflict—and caused much pain and death—but their existence among Europeans allowed and encouraged a certain amount of "free" and independent inquiry and provided for that people a good deal of conflicting theory and "facts" that stimulated among many of them an independent mind set that continues to this day to push them to investigate everything. Therefore, their willingness and ability to question the **known** as well as the **unknown** and not be totally dependendent upon the popular and accepted wisdom (religion or secular) has been a key aspect for European-American advancement. Also, we must understand that the West has never been immune to stealing or borrowing the state and commercial secrets of anybody and claiming ownership. Much of their development is based upon stolen or accumulated knowledge that existed for years in other parts of the world, e.g., the Chinese had gun power and steam and the Afrikans had iron, writing, math, astronomy, etc. (2) The second factor is that of the Europeans' concept of **Manifest Destiny**: White World Supremacy with their undying belief that they are **right, correct, best** and **good** in all things. They believe that their laws, values, history, psychology, justice, technology, religion, world view, i.e, their way of doing everything from love making to cooking monkey meat, is the one and only way. And this belief was/is so strong that they risk life, country and beliefs to carry them worldwide through both the word (bible) and the gun, regardless of the consequences to self and others. Realizing also that this was not only a political, economic and military venture, but above all, a cultural one (colonization). The forcing of their worldview on the world as well as the colonization of the people and resources of the world, gave Europe the edge it needed to complete its mission—that of world dominance through the controlling of world thought, i.e., through European culture manifested as World culture or more succinctly, Universalism.

III

Most people are hooked into a belief system. The major belief system that most Black people in America support and are committed to is Christianity. One of the problems with religious belief systems is that often they are opposed to rational thinking, that is if one is deeply involved with a certain belief it is difficult to acknowledge contradictions in that belief especially if it has been able to improve one's life at some level. Because of the influences of the various belief systems, there is a serious shortage of original and imaginative thinking around today's problems. It is often **easier to believe than think**. You may say that there are exceptions, yes, but for every Rev. Herbert Daughtry, there are five hundred to make small of him and his thoughts. The identity of Black people in the United States is a confusing affair because **the majority identify more closely with belief systems rather than historical roots or traditions**, therefore, it is not unusual for an Afro-American to define him/-herself as a Christian, Muslim, Hebrew, Buddhist,

Marxist, democrat or a member of the sugar hill gang rather than that which connects him/her to land, language, history or culture that represents his/her past or present condition.

At this point I must acknowledge the value of the thoughts and actions of Malcolm X, Hoyt Fuller and Bobby Wright—the importance of their lives to me has been their undying search for truth within truth, even if this truth opposes the popular conceptions of what is considered truth. Let me explain.

The way a people perceive the world and the way the world actually is, could be and often is, several different realities. Our perception (right or wrong) shape our actions and our actions are nothing more than the end results of our understanding of how we should act or react. Our perceptions grow out of our education and one's education is a production of a people's or nation's culture. A person's biology is also a determinant in how one observes the world but to the degree of its ultimate importance, vice versa, cultural influences are still open to question. However, it is safe to state that local and national cultures, in their most complete definitions continue to a large degree to shape the consciousness of all people irrespective of gender. But, by in large, the cultures of the world are male dominated and male directed; the female influences are present, but they are subtle and often openly subordinated to the direction and focus of male imperatives. However, the influences of females continue to be the most influential during a child's early years and come on strong again at mating time.

A limited male worldview may be part of the world's problems. A one sided view of the world often produces an arrogance and self righteousness that interferes with meaningful communication and if people cannot communicate in realistic terms; understanding and perceptions of reality are just about impossible. To understand a people, any people, study the culture. Every people, no matter how "advanced" or "misdeveloped" they may be—if we are to understand them in an intimate and non-superficial manner—we must go to the root of why they act or react a certain way to a given stimulus or situation, study the culture:

Why is it that the Hindus of India refuse to eat beef while many of them starve?

Why is it that Black People in the United States who on a daily basis endure unbelievable insult and oppression remain so forgiving toward their oppressors?

Why is it that the Moslems protest the eating of pork?

Why is that many of the world's people are vegetarians?

Why is it that in some cultures the women are circumsized and in others the men are and in some cultures circumcision doesn't exist?

Why are there so many religions where some people believe in one God and others believe in many, where some believe in witches and others in messiahs and blessed trinities?

Life is seldom random. There are reasons for all actions whether the reasons are obvious or not. The explanation for a particular action may not be to our liking, but that too is another question. The works of Cheikh Anta Diop, Marvin Harris, Ivan Van Sertima, Margaret Mead, Edward T. Hall, Harold Cruse, Frances Cress Welsing, Maulana Karenga and many others attest to the influences of culture. The main point is that the western way (which is often defined as being universal) is not the only way and may not be the best means of ascertaining answers to complex and sometimes seemingly unanswerable questions.

Answers as to why people act "odd" or "different" in other parts of the world or in closely corresponding communities often come from the misinformed, ethnic chauvinists, sophisticated racists or go unanswered. We are given traditional explanations like, "they have always done it that way", which is not an answer to why, but a limiting observation. In some cases we are given "religious" or "spiritual" explanations rather than down to earth material ones. This is not to suggest that the answers given in the local cultural or religious context are incorrect, but it is to suggest that there may be **more correct answers.** The rain and the sun in some cultures may be Gods or products of Gods, but also in other cultures there may be other answers to why the sun and rain exist.

The importance of knowing the practical day to day living situations, as well as the historical and geographical patterns of a people cannot be overly emphasized. The elements that develop consciousness (perceptions) are love, fear, conflict, ignorance and knowledge. Mystification of the world is most evident among powerless, landless, defenseless and misdeveloped people. A people who, for the most part, do not seek answers for their condition within themselves and their environment, but continue to read "tea leaves", study the "stars", or hang on the last words of so called "holy" men or women or fall back on such nonsense as "we always done it that way" are indeed, a people who will not advance or contribute much to self or world development.

Life may well be a theatre, but it is also much more than that which can be learned in drama classes. More often than not, a people's history depends on who writes it. Historical interpretations are not patented and like donuts, mixes vary with the amount of flour and sugar added. History is a monster and whether we get lies, truths or a combination, much of that which lives with us depends on whether we are the recorders or readers, conquerors or conquered. It is obvious that the **winners interpret the world.**

IV

A People Cannot Develop Unless They Have A Culture That Is Progressive and Life Giving

One of the major hindrances to our economic and political development is that on a mass level our major sources of life-giving and lifesaving information have, for the most part, been **negative.** Most of us, especially our children, as well as our parents, teachers, and professionals are products of a highly sophisticated negative information bank. Our lives do not revolve around the best knowledge available for serious development. Most of us secure our information via mass media (radio, t.v., newspaper, magazine), each other, our jobs, and failing educational systems.

Black people view more television and are dependent upon its information, to a larger extent, than any other ethnic group in the country. The Black viewing average is somewhere between 6 and 8 hours a day—watching t.v. is almost like a job. In fact many of our people organize their days and evenings around television. I did not realize the extent that young Black college students depend on t.v. until one day, while visiting a Black college student lounge around soap opera time. I was startled into a new realization which stimulated serious study; many of the students had organized their class schedules around their favorite soap opera.

Very seldom do we engage in primary research of any kind. Answers to our most complex problems come from the top of somebody's head or from secondary and interpreted sources. The western world's acculturation process has instilled in most of us a **culture of survival**. This limited survivalism has equipped most of us to seek the **easy way out**. Therefore, high school is a party, undergraduate studies are where we find mates and graduate school is where we may become serious—a good six years after others.

Over the last twenty years Black mis-education has been more effective than at anytime in our history. The evidence of this is blatantly obvious—the great majority of college graduates (about 500,000 since 1962), have not consistently been working in the best interest of Black people. This talent pool is about the best "educated" group of Black people in the world in the areas of mass communication, legal skills, and new technology; and they, the vast majority, do not collectively or individually work for the betterment of Black people.

No other Black people in the world can touch Black people in this country in the area of science and technology, yet Black people in the U.S. are worse off in terms of economic gains, political clout, living conditions than we were twenty years ago. The

question is why? The answer is frighteningly simple—-
Black people, as well as others, **do what we have
been taught to do.** The U.S. education system
(primary, secondary, and higher) has not taught us to
service Black peoples' needs, but has prepared us to
service the needs of IBM, GM, XEROX, ABC, CBS,
DuPont, etc. In fact, education for Black liberation is
hardly ever raised in a university setting in the United
States.* And if Black liberation is studied, it is in the
context of a pseudo-economic liberation which is
illusionary at best, and still dependent. Generally,
Black graduates from colleges in the country are
molded into one of seven categories:

1) **Non-functioning illiterates**: Cannot read, write,
compute, think or articulate their thoughts and have
no visible skills.

2) **Functional illiterates**: Can barely read and write to
where they may be able to perform the most minimal
of jobs in a technological country, such as cleaning
up.

3) **Functional literates:** First level paper pushing, can't
or don't think; Not creative—good at taking orders
and excellent at exaggerating their own importance.

4) **Patriotic literates:** Same as number 3 but will die
for the flag, country, local God, and General Motors.

5) **Frustrated Intellectuals:** Found mostly in the centers of higher education, often confusing merit with
quota and political expediency in terms of their
existence. Usually very detached from students and
are critically insecure, badly indebt and caught up in
the upwardly mobile rat race and generally die very
young or end up as chronic alcoholics or drug

* The exceptions would be where strong Black Studies Departments or programs exist.

addicts. Their brothers and sisters can also be found in the corporate world and in upper echelon government jobs. Generally these people's last original thought was at the age of six.

6) **Athletes, Entertainers, Preachers, Business People:** They can run faster, jump the highest, and sell 7-Up and Converse gym shoes with the greatest smiles since false teeth were invented. They can dance, sing, tell jokes, drop names, spend money and love hugging Johnny Carson. They talk to God daily and represent mis-guided self-centered leadership in the Black community. They are aspiring capitalists, they publish magazines, make hair oil, are mayors of cities, do independent consulting, head civil rights organizations and are without peer in articulating other people's thoughts on the problems of the Negro. All these people think that they are independent. Also they will sell their people without batting their eyes if the deal is right. Our leadership comes from this group.

7) **Liberated Intellectuals:** Small but growing body of brothers and sisters that view the uncompromising liberation of its people as a priority, and will use most of their talent and resources for that end. Malcolm X, Bobby Wright, Hoyt Fuller, Larry Neal, Bob Marley, and Fannie Lou Hamer were part of this tradition. Among those who continue in this direction are Maulana Karenga, John Henrik Clarke, Chancellor Williams, Yosef ben-Jochannan, Anderson Thompson, Gwendolyn Brooks, Jacob Carruthers, Frances Welsing, Lerone Bennett, Mari Evans, Sonia Sanchez, etc. This group is comprised of original thinkers and doers.

V

Coming Back to Life: Realistic Optimist

The question is can we develop among the majority of our people a movement whose ultimate objective is the **liberation** of Black people? The answer is a **qualified yes**. Yes, if we can reverse the negative aspects of this negative culture and revive the tradition of independent thought, action and work as we enlarge the ranks of **liberated intellectuals**.

Liberated intellectuals are not necessarily college graduates, but are people who find freedom in the investigation of ideas that are geared toward the betterment of life. The thrust for functional knowledge needs to be a way of life in our communities. Let me give you an example of a people who are knowledge seekers.

The Japanese,* who were soundly defeated and whose economy was virtually destroyed less than 40 years ago, have rebuilt themselves to the point that they vacillate between Number 1 and Number 3 economically in the world. Book after book marvel over the Japanese miracle. Yet, it is not a miracle. What the Japanese people have done is to recapture the Japanese cultural imperatives, and using the world as their university, have out worked, out thought, out produced the world that destroyed them in the last world war.

The Japanese live on an island about the size of Montana, with a population of 115,000,000 people, representing one of the most densely populated nations in the world. They import thirty percent of their food and have virtually no petroleum, iron ore, coal or other mineral resources. Therefore, these shortages necessitate that they import about 85% of their energy resources. Yet, with these obstacles, Tokyo, the world's most populated city, is absolutely

*See Ezra F. Vogel's *Japan As Number 1: Lessons for America*.

the cleanest, safest and most mobile. The Japanese economy, which less than 20 years ago, produced merchandise that people laughed at, is now the model for the industrialized west. No one is laughing anymore because they now control major markets that yesterday belonged to other countries: the watch industry was Swiss controlled; motorcycle manufactur ing was British; camera and lens production belonged to the Germans; optical equipment was German and American; musical instruments, especially pianos, were American; and the foundation of the American economy, the automobile, has also been dethroned by the Japanese.

The Japanese are also becoming dominant in the production of bicycles, ski equipment, stereo equip ment, zippers, ship building, etc. The field of aero-space technology is becoming a new area for the Japanese along with their control of the computer microchip.

The extraordinary versatility of the Japanese people can be found in their **unsavory belief in themselves.** They are ethnocentric, that is they see themselves as one people tied together by race, culture, land and traditions. They have their own land base and have made it work for them. They do not have a "race" problem to contend with. Most impor-tantly, for the nation, the pursuit of knowledge is the number one priority. The gathering of functional knowledge is one of the most important activities for individuals, families, organizations, and corporations. Knowledge has replaced capital as the most important resource. They gather information from everywhere, and study as a social activity continues throughout their lives. Their attitude toward strangers is, "What can I learn from them?"

Japan is one of the most literate nations in the world, and next to the United States, leads the way in the production of books, about 30,000 per year since W.W. II. There have been over 150,000 translations in the last 30 years. Their educational television teaches as well as entertains. Rather than argue over a problem, many seek more information and "smother a problem". One of the reasons that their society is so production orientated is because the profits of the public and private sectors are more evenly distributed than in the United States and the class differences are not as negatively emphasized as in the west. The scope of government and corporate information gathering is breath taking. Other facts include:

1) 90% of young people complete high school

2) A higher percentage of young people complete university education in Japan—about the highest in the world. Competition to get into the university is fierce.

3) Life expectancy is the highest in the world and there is a deep, deep respect for elders.

4) For an industrialized nation, Japan has one of the lowest infant mortality rates.

5) Its defense budget is one of the lowest in the industrialized world due to its defense agreement with the United States.

The key point is that the Japanese are one people caring about one another and their nation and have discovered the best way to beat the world is simply to know more and be able to use that knowledge more productively than others.

Black people in the United States have a deceptive knowledge base, especially among the so called conscious Black and political people. Generally, what you'll find is that a person is either Black and not political or political and not Black. **Very seldom do we see a sophisticated Black Cultural awareness steeped in political reality among our youth. There is confusion unending.** This is partially caused by the lack of a Black social theory that answers most questions of life and death for Black people.

Much of this confusion can be eradicated if we define the negative sources and extradite ourselves from their influences. I've singled out the mass media and the acculturation process. Now, let me issue another warning: **We have to stop being mesmerized by so called Black leadership.** For the most part, our leadership is self-appointed or selected for us by others. If a comparison of white western world leadership and Black western world leadership is made, one can easily see that unless change is made almost immediately, we will continue in a no win situation.

The following chart illustrates the two leaderships that influence our lives on a daily basis.

White Western World Leadership [white men]
A. Business Men

B. Politicians

C. Military

D. Intellectual sector—mainly research and development Science and Technology

Support Group
E. Religion

F. Education

G. Communication

H. Sports and Entertainment

I. Other

Black Western World Leadership [Black men]

A. Black male ministers

Support Group

B. Business men

C. Sport figures

D. Entertainers

E. Politicians

F. Educators

G. Others

We are out maneuvered at every turn because our leadership for the most part has been trained either directly or indirectly by white western world leadership to be mainly moral and spiritual men. Black male ministers cannot effectively deal with white business men who are about one world economy, who plan to take off countries while our leadership seeks the biggest and finest churches in the country. We fail to deal effectively with white politicians because they are about controlling the world—will kiss your baby in the morning and issue a contract on your life at night. Our response to the military has been ludicrous—we collect Black people's weapons and turn them in while whites build ever more sophisticated killing machines. The military in this country doesn't pray, doesn't negotiate, they will follow orders and take you off the earth anyway you want to go: quietly or loudly. And finally, our leadership is anti-intellectual. They refuse to question the known or unknown; have no research and development arm to speak of, and refuse to read a book outside of their discipline, unless it is on the required reading list at the University of Chicago Divinity School. This element of Black leadership is mainly self serving, economically greedy, and insecure. Examples of their treachery or naivete' are unbounded. Black people are by circumstances seekers of a better way of life. This may explain why hundreds gave up their lives and possessions in the United States and followed Jim Jones (a white minister) to Guyana pursuing the the good life and earthly peace.

Many people are still trying to understand Jonestown. Reluctantly, we try to digest a nightmare and its horrible aftermath. After millions of words and countless explanations from clergy, news media, scholars and street corner philosophers, one would have been utterly isolated not to have been touched by the sheer horror of such an event. That the great majority of those murdered were Black people gives to us no small lesson, if we choose to accept it. The lesson: Stop believing in men and women waving "spiritual" books promising the universe; start studying, thinking and evaluating the world as rationally as possible, especially those things pertaining to one's own cultural, spiritual, political and material development; actively take hold of one's own life, rather than give it up to forces outside comprehension or control.

Not so suddenly, Black people in America have become a nation of joiners. Too often we blindly follow without critically assessing that to which we give our time. money and creative talents. The entities that we give our allegiance to the great majority of the time are not political organizations, block clubs, food co-ops, progressive social organizations, study groups or military organizations. Our support, whole heartedly and uncritically, goes to the Black church (and sometimes white church) plus an assortment of Negro social and fraternal organizations. That we are the first the seekers of spiritual fulfillment and enlightenment is not unusual. Many wish to dismiss our Afrikan connection, but undoubtedly it can best be seen and understood once the Afrikan spiritual association is made. Sometimes it is easy to forget and quite tempting to play down the role of the Black Church; however, other than bars, taverns, liquor stores, restaurants, beauty and barber shops, undertakers and a few civil rights and social organizations, the Black church remains the largest and most influential spiritual-social-business institution in the Black community today. That it is not more effective today only speaks to the conservatism of its leadership and the backwardness of much of its philosophical teachings.

Indeed, one can say without much apprehension that if the church does not change, its future in the Black community (in this rapidly changing world) may be limited. However, for the moment there is no great danger of the demise of the Black church. The danger exists in the church's negative response to the destruction of Black people by a system which cares little about moral responsibility and nothing about a people outside its racial and cultural family. The Black church, civil rights and social organizations' traditional response to this danger has been one of **turning the cheek and blaming the victim.** It has also been one of encouraging among the people a consciousness of **quiet submission.**

If rapid and progressive change does not occur soon among Black people, we will continue to grow politically and culturally empty and weak, posturing as a people, but who are actually zombies who follow and join, who color and copy, who buy and buy and who find greater pleasure in working for the enemies of our people than in working for ourselves.

It was not foolish rhetoric or idealistic nonsense when the white world moved to remake the world in its own image. Such control could only be lasting if one dominated, 1) Cultural reality; 2) Commerce; 3) Armament development and manufacture. However, the lasting effect of European control was to be felt the greatest in the destruction of the Afrikan mind. The Psychology of Afro-American people as it exists today is a product of European-American Culture.

Culture

As a people, our understanding of culture is severely limited. Black culture as a force for survival and development is given very little attention in the education of our young. However, the education that is transmitted (or not transmitted) is a product of the culture. The politics and the economics that a people experience do not just appear, but are the unique results of that people's or somebody else's culture. The language as well as the science and technology that bring meaning (or control) to a people's life is also cultural.

One problem, of course, is that to most of us culture as a concept is abstract—that is one does not actually observe culture. Yet we all experience its manifestations, such as: clothing, art, music, housing, weapons, films, literature, political and social organizations, food, educational organizations, economic structures, etc. Anthropologist Laura Thompson sees culture as

...the supreme creation of a human community, the product of its deep seated urge to fulfill and perpetuate itself...it is primarily a group problem-solving device instituted by a human community to cope with its basic practical problems.

Dr. Thompson places great emphasis on culture as **coping** and problem-solving. However, it must be noted that there exists among anthropologists and sociologists differences of opinion as to conclusive definitions of culture. Edward T. Hall in his **Beyond Culture** states that most serious students of culture however,

> ...do agree in three characteristics of culture: it is not innate, but learned; the various facets of culture are interrelated—you touch a culture in one place and everything else is shared and in effect defines the boundaries of different groups.

Hall goes on to point out that

> ...Culture is man's medium; there is not one aspect of human life that is not touched and altered by culture. This means personality, how people express themselves (including shows of emotion), the way they think, how they move, how problems are solved, how their cities are planned and laid out, how transportation systems function and are organized, as well as how economic and government systems are put together and function.

My focus on culture is to clear the air of serious misconceptions in regard to cultural influence and to hopefully move our analysis beyond the trap of looking at race, politics and economics as isolated and non-related entities. The way a people view themselves and the extent to which they rise up out of any situation and decide their own course is a serious cultural question. Culture "shared understanding", is that medium in which values are transmitted from generation to generation. It is generally accepted that human behavior can be and is systematically observed and that the variability of individuals is a result of inherited characteristics (biology) and life experience (culture).

In the United States today several negative developments are quite evident among our people as a result of a negative cultural impact:

1) Much of the Black youth (especially Black males) are without positive guidance and are therefore potentially dangerous to themselves and their communities. Young Black men who frequently just "hang out" are feared in the community and those parents who are responsible for them are generally unable to exert control.

2) Blacks, especially in the highly congested and overcrowded urban areas, are more and more accepting the negative aspects of European-American culture. The increase in violence and recreational sex are examples.

3) The Black intellectual class has still not answered the major questions of life, death and existence for Black people in America as Black people. In fact, one of the self-defeating characteristics of the Black intellectual class is that too often its roots are not Black but white painted black.

4) There is no local, state or nationwide defense mechanism for the Black community.

5) Black male/female relationships are at an all time low. The deliberate move by the dominant culture to disrupt family life and its conscious efforts to make Black men obsolete is fast becoming a reality.

6) The Black view of the world has become too limiting. We are too instant-oriented.

7) True and binding love is fastly fading from our communities.

8) Black on Black crime is at a serious all-time high.

9) We allow and sometimes encourage incompetents to lead us. There. is no accountability for our leadership.

10) A serious lack of substantial life-giving, life-saving and life-sustaining institutions in the Black community is evident.

11) Our children are **not** priority.

12) There exists no national or local communication network.

13) The use of drugs—legal and illegal is rampant in the Black community. There is severe dependency on artificial stimuli.

14) The Black business class has not begun to even consider the economics of the Black community.

15) Too many Black babies are having babies; therefore, a dangerous cycle is in motion among our youth where sexual expression is equated with manhood and womanhood, and all too often, young people who find themselves with children, end up participat-

ing in the destruction of themselves and their children.

16) Education is not a priority in our community ay any level. There is absolutely no understanding of functional economics; politics is a word game played by would be high-rollers, and our current skills bank is obsolete in this scientific and technological state.

17) The desolution of the family is epidemic.

VI

Culture and Consciousness

A people's consciousness, the way they view and operate in the world, is shaped by their (or another's) culture. All of the answers are not in; however, it seems that culture can disable and kill as well as develop and give life. The most prevailing consciousness among most Black people today is one of survival. And this survival is not of a collective nature where individuals, communities and institutions work together to solve problems. Black survival, especially in the urban areas, is more Darwinian, a "survival of the fittest" attitude. Its proponents will use whatever means at their disposal to achieve their end regardless of the cost and pain to others.

It has often been stated that Black people in America represent the revolutionary vanguard. Indeed, we may be a vanguard—but revolutionary, we are not. That is, if I understand the concept of revolutionary vanguard as a people who are bold and sophisticatedly violent while actively involved in replacing an unjust, corrupt system with one that is just and uncorruptible, and working for the people. The evidence does not support this, no matter how we wish to romanticize today's "revolutionary climate". If any climate exists it is one of de-revolution. The political/educational/military/financial organizations of the United States have been actively involved, especially in the last twenty years, through the use of mass media, politics, sports and entertainment in de-politicizing millions of Black people.

Ask the average Black to articulate what he or she wants out of life and you will get about the same answers the white middle class would give. However, for the great majority of Blacks who are not able to move to Black middle-classism, they end up settling for what they can get. Therefore, we have been forced into, as well as help develop, a **Culture of Survival**—not one of **Development**. The survival culture deals more with immediate needs rather than long-term needs. The on-going search for food, shelter, clothing, sex, material artifacts, social status and fast week-ends are what direct us and absorb our energies on a day-to-day basis. As a result, there exists very little time for serious development. Yet, the most hurting aspect of this is that if the time existed, there would still be few examples of genuine development.

The culture of survival breeds people who riot rather than plan revolution. It develops people who re-act rather than act, beg rather than take, play rather than study and follow rather than lead. Let's take a closer look at two cultural mentalities: 1) The revolutionary or progressive mentality is one that builds and creates and works for the long-term; 2) the riot mentality is one of instant-gratification, more destructive than constructive. The revolutionary would take over a school system or build a school while the rioter would burn the school down and give little thought to the results of that action.

The following chart is designed to more clearly characterize these two mentalities as they affect our development as a people:

MAXIMUM CULTURAL DEVELOPMENT
Revolutionary Mentality

1. Study oriented: reads, evaluates and debates books, newspapers, magazines and scholarly journals.
2. Worker: looks for ways in which to actively work for self—may hold a job outside in order to sustain self and family.
3. Organized and systematic.
4. Progressively collective; conscious of others.
5. Family-oriented, regards mate as partner in struggle; loves children.
6 Land consciousness—realizes that the only thing that nobody is making any more of is land.
7. Disciplined. Strong and unyielding.
8. Serious.
9. Analytical and critical.
10. Frugal—buys mainly on need basis.
11. Social life is developmental and involves children.
12. Creatively aggressive—will dare the impossible, if it is productive.
13. Respects elders.
14. Dislikes incompetence and mediocrity.
15. Fights against Black on Black crime. Understands that the root of Black on Black crime is white on Black crime.

16. Loves Black art/music and literature.

17. Can give and follow instructions.

18. Committed to Black liberation.

19. No drug use.

20. Politically active, not crisis oriented, acts on information rather than reacts.

21. Self-confident. Respects others regardless of race or culture.

22. Understands the economic forces that control our lives on a local, national, as well as international level.

SURVIVAL CULTURAL EXISTENCE
Accommodationist/Riot Mentality

1. Does not **read** or **study** after "formal" education. Buys few books, reads mainly newspapers, sports pages or popular novels and magazines.

2. Works eight-hours for someone else. Welfare conscious—get it for nothing attitude.

3. Unsystematic and definitely not organized unless it is for someone else.

4. Backwardly individualistic—I, me, mine mentality.

5. Not family oriented. Regards mate as property. Lowrates children. Generally, single minded; does not want children or responsibility of homelife.

6. Not land conscious.

7. Non-disciplined, actively fights against discipline.

8. Non-serious majority of time.

9. Not critical or analytical. Prefers not to think for self.

10. Consumer junkie—if it's advertised, they got it. Cannot distinguish wants from needs.

11. Loves social and night life, i.e., lives for the weekend, loves sexual conquests.

12. A defeatist—few goals other than acquisition of material artifacts.

13. Puts elders in nursing homes and forgets them.

14. Gravitates towards incompetence and mediocrity.

15. Involved in Black on Black crime—or apathetic to the issue.

16. Loves music of the new generation—any kind.

17. Can give instructions but not follow them.

18. Committed to self-liberation only.

19. Drug dependency—cigarettes, alcohol, hard drugs, etc.

20. Politically inactive. Crisis oriented. Reacts.

21. Egotistical, ignorantly arrogant, has little concept of culture; feel they are forever racial underclass.

22. Naive of economics, unaware of the international nature of capitalism that touches all of our lives.

This comparison is not scientific. But it represents my conception of the highest and the most destructive responses of two opposing cultural orientations. It is obvious that there cannot be progress ,without a progressive and revolutionary culture working at its highest level. The rebellions of the sixties were both reactive and proactive. Much of the destruction that took place in the sixties was in the Black community. There are concrete reasons for this and if we are to move forward we have to confront the truth. As I see it, the reasons that most Blacks don't struggle at a political level are:

1) Many Black people are **satisfied** with the way their lives are and fear radical change from any segment of society.

2) Of those Black people that believe change is necessary, many don't know what to do about it and feel that their individual efforts are not worth much; therefore, they do nothing but talk.

3) Just about every Black family in the country has one or more personal traumas that they are dealing with that consumes their quality time, e.g., a son or husband in prison; a mother or family member seriously ill; basic economic survival, etc.

4) In most Black families its members can point to at least one family member, no matter how remote, who has "made it" in America and that person(s) is constantly used as the example of what we all can do with hard work, fortitude, initiative, etc. This implies that Black failure is always individually instituted.

5) A great many young Black adults are interacting on a day to day basis with white people either at school, work or play and find it difficult to separate the evils that the white race has perpetuated against Blacks and others with their new found friendships. Somehow the one or two white friends or mates exonerate the crimes of their people. Therefore, to many Blacks "people are just people" and organized white death squads fall in the category of unbelievability and a historical perspective of Black-white confrontations is generally unknown or dismissed.

6) The failure of Black leadership to accurately inform.

Therefore, it is clear that our cultural models must be sophisticated as well as revolutionary. The

Culture of Accommodation; Submission and Riot is encouraged and glorified in the United States. The Cult of Material Acquisition is normal and those that reject such obvious nonsense are regarded as abnormal. Therefore, we are encouraged and indeed rewarded with trinkets and positions of pseudo-responsibility, if we seek the "American Dream" through the avenues of Survival Cultural Orientation.

Cultural-Spiritual-Historical-Political Autonomy

Numerically, in the United States, Black people are strong. However, politically we are weak and fragmented. Split by superficial differences often imposed from the alien outside. We, who are without a national land base must, therefore, pull from the forces within us that will act as catalysts and energizers. Since land is not the unifying force for us at this time, greater attention must be given to a political-cultural-spiritual-historical base that is not solely dependent upon territory. Black Culture as a living force is a product of each generation. That is, we develop from existing culture and in the process we produce new additions to the traditional culture. The two greatest weapons used against the development of a strong cultural-spiritual-historical base have been, 1) Assimilation: e.g., integration, more rhetoric than real; 2) Elimination: the strong majority and its leadership that would not buy assimilation has been ruthlessly contained and/or sometimes quietly taken off the earth.

Cultural-political-spiritual-historical autonomy at its best speaks to the collective personality of a people and is clearly demonstrated in that people's ability to resist destructive elements from wherever they arise. A living Black nation is not solely dependent upon a land base for it to strive and develop. Under ideal conditions, yes—one's own land is precious and critically important. However, Black people in the United States, who may be landless by the year 1985, have a strong national will to survive and—to a degree— unite. What is missing is a **vision** beyond the syndrome of "making it in America".

VII

Memory as Development

One of the reasons that Jewish people, against great odds, have not been erased from the earth is because they refused to relinquish memory. As a people they developed a mythology, both sacred and secular, of their people and tenaciously practiced the bonding traditions, both privately and publicly. Traditions are catalytic; they act as solder and glue, holding people together under the most horrid conditions. Whether the enemy is fire or water, man or beast, the mythology (i.e., the foundation of the culture) must be steel-like. The only sure way of destroying that people is to wipe the earth dirty with them, grinding their bones into fertilizer. But as long as a people, any people, can hang on to and develop along the lines directed by the sunlight of their foreparents, there is hope. When any people's direction is not in keeping with the dictates of the ruling sector, the cementing factor for the outsider is culture, i.e., functional knowledge manifesting itself along with the best of their traditions.

When a people or nation has it's own cultural imperatives and they are manifested effectively every second throughout the nation, it becomes extremely difficult to disrupt the lives of such people. Due to cultural reinforcement, world Jewry, speaking in the skins of liberals, conservatives, laborers, comics, or scientists, orthodox or reform, have one unrelenting

154

mind set: **Freedom as Jews.** Isaiah Berlin in his **Against the Current**, states it this way;

> All Jews who are at all conscious of their identity as Jews are steeped in history. They have longer memories, they are aware of a longer continuity as a community than any which has survived. The bonds that unite them have proved stronger than the weapons of their persecutors and detractors; and stronger than a far more insidious weapon; the persuasions of their own brothers, fellow Jews who, at times, with much sincerity and skill try to argue that these bonds are not as strong or as peculiar as they seem; that the Jews are united by no more than a common religion or common suffering; that their differences are greater than their similarities and therefore that a more enlightened way of life—liberal, rationalist, socialist, communist—will cause them to dissolve peacefully as a group into their social and national environment—that at most their unity may come to be no greater than that of say Unitarians, Buddhists, vegetarians, or any other world wide group, sharing certain common, not always too passionately held, convictions. If this had been true, there would not have been enough vitality, not enough desire to live a common life, to have made colonization of Palestine, and ultimately the state of Israel, possible. Whatever other factors may have entered in to the unique amalgam which, if not always Jews themselves, at any rate the rest of the world instantly recognizes as the Jewish people, historical consciousness—sense of continuity with the past—is among the most powerful.

I may not agree with Zionist politics as manifested on

the world stage; however, I do respect the Jewish people's desire to define and execute their worldview against great odds.

A Black national vision will emerge only if a people's cultural apparatus is functioning overtime pointing in such a direction. Collective culture will forge collective personalities i.e., individuals working together, and thus move the minds of our people toward a movement that is people-centered. The question of an **Autonomous Destiny** (liberation) will only be asked if a people can **first** view themselves as a **people. A Black national vision is produced by able and sophisticated cultural institutions, a strong and visible Black media, a resourceful and applied collective language, superior schools, safe and secure homes, working churches, adequate financial resources, powerful defense force, an active Eldership, work-oriented people, uncorruptible values, and able intelligentsia, and masses of people who will involve themselves in a rebuilding process.**

The strengths of the cultural apparatus will determine the degree to which alien assimilation is successful. The cultural-spiritual-historical apparatus is the protective shield of any people and is responsible for the development of "inner strengths" that continually, at an individual level, combat assimilation, negativeness and elimination. The ego or collective will of a nation is best displayed in a people's interaction with each other as well as the alien outside. That is—do a people look after each other, do they share at a high level (material and otherwise), are they responsible for each other's children, are they continually creative in relationships, etc? However, once a people travel outside their own culture, they must be sophisticated enough to make certain adaptations to the alien's culture which will allow the alien culture (white) or other, to work for them. **Therefore, it is necessary that we be bicultural in the sense that we understand and can maneuver in the alien culture as the same culture attempts to destroy us.**

VIII

Why the Black Church is Successful and its Effect on Memory

As mentioned earlier, it is far easier to believe than think. It has not always been that way, but let's deal with what is. Most of our people are organized around religious beliefs rather than race or cultural beliefs. These religious beliefs are diverse and varied, which is to say that if Black people cannot unify around a God, why is it that we think Black people will unify around progressive ideas?

The success of the modern Black church to a large degree rests on the shoulders of Black women. The women build the churches and the men run them. It is also clear that the Black church is the only bastion of power in the Black community where Black men can excel and not be internally challenged by white men. Today's Black church is a safe haven for Black male development as long as that church doesn't challenge white male dominance in the nation.

The major building construction in Black communities is being initiated by the churches, which means that the church is growing. The assets of the Black church in Chicago exceed one billion dollars and is escalating. Some reasons for the strength of the church in the Black communities are:

1) The Black church has come to represent tradition and history is, therefore, **legitimate and right**, receiving aid from both advocates and enemies.

2) For the most part, the church is **not** political,

therefore, it is safe, and if it does allow politics into its walls, you can be sure it will be safe politics. Of course, there are exceptions—however, the average church goer relishes this non-involvement of the church in political matters that might harm its existence.

3) The minister tells a good story that connects members to each other and to a brighter future. Believers can get happy in the church, let loose on their dreams without being belittled.

4) Church music refreshes and renews. The music uplifts while portraying better times. The music moves the bones, energizes the blood and induces new spirit into the body.

5) Spiritually, the instillation of the spirit allows some to make it from week to week, year to year, giving members the strength to overcome most things human and inhuman.

6) The church provides clear, no nonsense answers to life and death questions.

7) The church reinforces important values such as the family and the patriarchy while accenting an acceptable morality and traditional values.

8) The church provides that which is considered the great truths, the ultimate enlightment and of course, through baptism and commitment, one is given entry into the next world.

The ministers of the great majority of the Black churches do not encourage their members to study anything other than the Bible and biblical commentary. Therefore, cultural and historical memory is only what one can interpret from the Bible. The average Black church goer and supporter seldom buy, or read materials not suggested by the minister or other church members. Most Black churches do not force its members to confront reality in any organized manner other than that which it sanctions. It must be remembered that any outside work takes the members away from building the church and, of course, doing God's work. Whether there is meaningful change in this situation depends on the actions of the current leadership. Many came of age in the sixties.

However, it can be said that the way of the Black church will be the way of a significant number of Black people. Religion, along with nationalism, remains one of the greatest forces in history. Religion also represents one of the key defining aspects of culture. What is needed is a Black Theology that totally works for the Black interest.

IX

Black Women and Male Culture

The unplanned and "matter of fact" misuse and abuse of women exist in most cultures. The issue of relegating the female to procreation and housework is a universal one. The west has sought to answer the question by providing an economy that demands that all work if they are to eat. Whereas the white females' entrance into the economy, according to Marvin Harris in **American Now**, displaced Black male workers and in effect hurt the economics of the Black family unit. Most Black women have had to work, and therefore, the relationship with their men around working has been somewhat different. Some of the problems in stable Black homes begin to surface when Black men lose jobs and cannot find new employment.

It is axiomatic that a sexist culture will produce a sexist mind. To deny that sexism exists is to deny we breathe. No matter how enlightened one thinks he or she is, this sexism seeps into our actions daily. However, it is obvious that for the enlightened, there are few jobs that men do that women cannot do. Cross cultural studies have indicated that time and time again—work that women perform is not necessarily their choice, but is culturally imposed and that in most cultures males dominate the cultural defining process.

As we move into the 21st century, especially in a highly scientific and technological society that has moved from a labor intensified economy to one that functions with computers and technology, the distinctions between men and women's work will evaporate. If the work place is able to move to an enlightened state, perhaps similar actions will prevail in the home. While spending three years in the United States Army, I learned a great lesson. I, as well as all other men, had to make our bed, clean our work and sleep areas, do kitchen duty and perform other acts that had been defined, by this culture, as women's work. It seems to me that if we could do "so called women's work" in the army, why can't we do it in civilian life, especially if our mates are working full time jobs also. It is insensitive and callous for men to expect their wives, often working eight hours, to come home and cook the food, clean the apartment, feed the children and husband, do the dishes, mop the floors, wash the clothes, etc. I'm sure you understand my point. If Black women are to advance and develop, they need time for self-realization, also the sharing of housework is not a negative comment on a man's masculinity, but an affirmation of a man's sense of fairness, love and security.

The bottom line is this—if we are to develop as people, the enlightened education requires that gender distinctions be minimized to those areas where such distinctions are vital and necessary. Understand that I am not pushing for a gender free society, but a society in which one is not oppressed due to sex, race, religion, etc. It is obvious that women cannot be replaced as mothers and men as fathers without serious and often detrimental disruptions of the family. **The family is priority** and one must be clear that the ideal family structure is one where partners (men and women) communicate—parenting and home duties are not predefined as something only women do. Serious development is a family activity that must include all members of the family.

X

Power, Politics and Force

International politics are complicated and often confusing. Language and cultural differences among nations add to the difficulty of communicating accurately. The recent (1982) Falkland crisis has made a law of international relations abundantly clear and definitive. In most power plays what really counts in the final analysis is unadulterated brute force aimed at the heart of your opponent. Power has little to do with being good, right or humane.

This observation can also be applied to the ever present Israel, PLO, Lebanon conflict where in the fall of 1982, Israel out-gunned, out-maneuvered and out killed all comers in its continued quest for land and recognition. Yet the Falklands, those dots of rock that frequent the South American coast, were until the armed conflict, the least expected hot spot on earth. Its lesson lies not in the land itself but the responses of Britain and Argentina. England won the war with a little help from her friends.

Neither Argentina nor Britain has a historical, moral or legal claim to the Falklands. Nor does South Afrika, the United States or Canada have valid claims to the land they now occupy. The USSR does not have rights to East Germany, Hungary, The Ukraine or the long stretches of land along its border with the People's Republic of China. It is increasingly clear that Poland and Afghanistan are in the Soviet orbit not due to democratically held elections. Most of the national borders of Afrika are not culturally or historically drawn but were left by European colonialists. These artifically imposed borders remain a source of conflict on the Afrikan continent. Witness recent fighting in Nigeria, Chad, Ethiopia, Uganda, Algeria, etc. Black people in the United States will never achieve parity with whites unless the world power imbalance is realized and corrected. Power is the only equal opportunity employer; the acquisition and use of force is raceless, classless, castless, sexless and only discriminates against those who do not have it.

Under the accepted order of things, if a government or group can grab, hold and develop a piece of land, it is theirs and can be challenged only by those who are more powerful and do not agree with such actions. The choice, as Albert Camus has noted, is not between good and bad, but between evil and lessor evil. As it has been said, "Power concedes only to power", moral outrage and prayers to gods and angels in response to evil do not play well with the marines or as the Afrikan proverb states, "A wise people know who to love and when to arm and organize."

XI

Crime

When a Black woman is raped and/or killed by a Black man; when a Black home is robbed or a Black person is mugged by Blacks, the analysis of the crimes committed by Blacks against Blacks is often that of the victim. The cry, which is often impassioned, is generally an indictment of the entire Black race. The physical and psychological damage served on Blacks by Blacks in the act of crime in the United States on a daily basis is incalculable. However, several things are certain. Black on Black crime exists and is growing. This crime works against Black unity and its existence is at epidemic levels and aids the enemies of Black people.

We can trace the root of such crime and attribute it to four factors; 1) Unusually high Black male unemployment, especially among the young—ages fourteen to thirty-four, and the concentration of this unemployment in areas that are racially isolated, economically depressed and "unprotected". 2) The dissolution of the Black nuclear and extended family, leaving us with over 60% of today's Black families headed by Black women who find it extremely difficult to meet day to day needs and are increasingly unable to give direction to or control the negative actions of young male children. Young Black males in high crime areas have few options other than the gang structure and dispirited schools. 3) The failure of the educational system to positively stimulate and direct young aggressive energies and provide them with the basic skills needed in a technological society. Miseducation in the U. S. has instilled in Black youth, mainly male, the desire to seek the easy way out. The important molders of behavior such as mass media, peer groupings, family, church, state, etc. are pointing young Black males toward destruction. 4) The failure of the political and social policies of the local and federal governments in providing support systems that lead toward prevention of crime rather than encouragement. The national crime policies are currently pro-crime and anti-Black developments.

Today's Black laborer is generally unskilled and

obsolete, and therefore, does not represent a productive labor pool in the current economy. This position has pushed many Blacks into an underground economy that is often "illegal" and very dangerous. The **question is this**—if a man or woman cannot feed, clothe, house or educate their children, where is the future? Where is the hope? Most people would lose confidence in a system that continuously contradicts its stated high ideals and continually works against the self-interest of that people. Self-preservation demands that a person, regardless of the conditions, do what he or she feels is best for them and their loved ones. When all else fails, crime becomes a serious option. Most Black people who commit crimes are not culturally conscious (race conscious) or political and therefore do not see the damage sustained by such actions.

Daily we are inundated with the vastness and richness of the country. Politicians are elected on anti-crime tickets and the mass media blinds us with violence and anti-social behavior. The largest area of crime, **white collar crime**, either goes unreported or is plea bargained down to where the offenders do little or no time. When a Richard Nixon or other high public or private officials can go free after committing **great** crimes, it sets in motion a moral climate that condones "little" crimes. To preach to the young about the evils and dangers of criminal activity is like talking to **loaded tanks.** The criminal practices of corporate capitalism are not only condoned, but are rewarded with tax payers' monies and deregulation. What people see here is a double standard of justice and downright dishonesty.

The economics of the country, as well as its political and social institutions, has created a functioning Black underclass that is concerned, like everyone else, with "making it" and over coming their current economic condition. **White on Black Crime** has forced Blacks to seek and be active in numerous economic areas even if such activity negatively impacts on Black people. The economic policies of the nation range from cuts in school lunch programs, day care services, food stamps, job corp, etc—these cuts are only the tip of the ball point pen—the damage that such cuts produce does not surface immediately but come at us like nightmares in between missed meals. Again, Black benefits are cut and the defense budget is almost doubled.

Any people whose existence has been reduced to survival does not think "rationally" or long and hard about their actions as they relate to Black advancement, struggle or development. As it is, Black people are caught in a catch 22 situation and are running towards permanent destruction as we bang our heads between empty pockets and a "keep the course" mentality. As long as Black on Black crime (by definition) only harms Blacks and poor people, little will be done other than public condemnation by city hall and Black leadership. According to the research of Richard Neely in his **The Politics of Crime**, only when violent crime seeps into the white middle, uppermiddle and upper classes will they be taken seriously, thus forcing the release of the resources of those classes to erase such crime by any means **deemed** appropriate.

It is obvious that we, the victims, must not sit and wait on others. One of the first acts of any self determining people is the protection and policing of themselves. Most other national groupings in the country do not depend upon outsiders to ensure the safety of their families. Crime remains an effective political weapon that is continuously used to stop progressive movement in its tracks. We must not continue to **react** and wait for city hall to bring forth solutions:

1) We need an immediate halt to the destruction of Black families. This means that (a) examples of stable families have to exist; (b) Family-making has to be taught; (c) Young people should be discouraged from getting married at an early age; (d) all our institutions should stress the emotional, economic and political benefits of strong Black families; (e) Black families currently in difficulty should seek adequate family counseling; (f) family support networks (indigenous and state supplied) need developing.

2) Black families should be non-violent. Domestic violence, whatever the reason should be outlawed. The increasing problem of battered women, among our people, coupled with all forms of rape that often go unreported has to be dealt with; (a) Conscious men need to help unconscious men, e.g., workshops, sports outings, clubs, etc; (b) Shelters for battered women and children need to be supported; (c) Help for Black men unable to control their aggression toward mates and children is needed.

3) The great majority of our **art** and **creative production** must stress; (a) strong families; (b) self-respect, self-reliance and self-protection; (c) the love of self and one's people; (d) the need for functional education at all ages; (e) strong political involvement and; (f) institutional development, e.g., schools, churches,. political clubs, social clubs, self-defense units, etc. It is clear that we must create a mass Black media that can turn the negative tide of the mass white media.

4) We have to organize and demand full employment, better housing and quality education that will prepare us for the 21st century. It is also clear that we can't totally be dependent upon the state for all of our

needs, therefore, we must always be seeking alternatives to what is "given" to us.

5) Strong innovative young adult programs need to be instituted immediately. Our youth are forever looking for productive programs but there are very few. Structured **youth** development in an atmosphere of love and discipline is urgently needed.

6) The adult and juvenile justice system needs a complete overhaul. Youthful aggression and violence are learned behavior and their existence cannot be blamed totally on the "women headed households" or the lack of male presence. What is missing is an all encompassing **developmental environment where adequate support systems** exist. This is a national problem, it is the Federal Government's responsibility to aid in the development of "social policies and intervention procedures" that will support new family structures.

Effective political and social organizing is all but impossible if we do not rebuild from the inside. Strong families are key to the fighting of crime as well as to the building of a strong people. The answers are not as difficult as we would like them to be. Much work has already been produced in this area, it is imperative that the National Associations of Black Social Workers and Black Psychologists join hands and minds and design programs that will positively impact on our people. Remember, it is naive to talk about a strong Black defense force if we cannot protect ourselves from each other.

XII

Futuretrends

This is a warning and a call for new preparation. We have entered the post-industrial age. Home computers are becoming common place for the middle class, and in the best secondary schools, the micro-computer and hand calculator have replaced much human instruction and the slide rule. New age technological systems, from health care to food production, have become more complex and their impact on our lives is often far-reaching and undesirable. Limited government regulations of hightech has helped to curb the negative excesses. However, the control of much of the new technology, such as genetic research, is left to the experts and the marketplace.

Colin Norman, in **The God That Limps: Science and Technology in the Eighties,** acknowledges that "technical change, in short, is a political process that cannot be separated from the broader forces operating in society". At this moment there is not a large public participation in, "the decisions that lead to the generation and adaptation of new technologies" and Black participation and understanding is just about nil. Technological evolution, unlike biological evolution, is often outside of one's immediate day to day experiences. For example, much of the technological development in the West is the result of government and corporate cooperation. One of the major reasons that solar technology has not developed at the pace of nuclear technology is that the sun's use as a military weapon is too costly.

Space, weapons, health care and law enforcement technologies are supported and motivated by different areas of society. Economics continues to impact on new technology primarily because the commercial forces are forever looking for ways to cut cost and maximize profits. Robots are now used in Japan in jobs that humans found dull, unrewarding and depressing. The field of Production Technology is about to radically alter the work place. The point is, technology can serve as well as harm. The degree that a people are informed and organized is directly related to whether a people become servants or masters of technology. In 1982 over $150 billion was invested in research and development with the majority being allocated to military and space research. It is obvious that Afrikans and people of color worldwide would have difficulty matching such commitments. Yet, in all systems regardless of complexity, there are contradictions and negatives. It is clear that we have to stop **reacting** and start directing our energies toward maximizing our understanding of this new world.

One avenue is to become aware of alternatives to high-tech. By no means is this to suggest that all high technology is of a backward nature, however, the thrust should be towards developing a technology that is people centered and resource conservative. Robot usage, in other than the most hazardous jobs, becomes disfunctioning in a society that has an extremely large and unemployed population. E.F. Schumacher, in his **Small is Beautiful: Economics As If People Mattered,** introduced many to the concept of AT (Appropriate Technology). I cannot do the impossible and define AT because the definitions by proponents and opponents are varied and many; however, it is safe to state that Schumacher was visualizing a technology that works for a people in concert with their environmental needs.

The other avenue is to try, as non-professionals, to stay as up to date as possible to the trends of the future and the role technology will play in it. One of the best and most recent books on future studies is **Megatrends: Ten New Directions Transforming Our Lives** by John Naisbett. The ten major shifts of the American Society as he sees them are:

1) From an industrial society to an information society.

2) From forced technology to high tech/high touch.

3) From national economy to a world economy.

4) From short-term to long-term.

5) From centralization to decentralization.

6) From institutional help to self-help.

7) From representative democracy to participatory democracy.

8) From hierarchies to networking.

9) From north to south.

10) From either/or to multiple options.

Mr. Naisbitt's **Megatrends** are not without critics, but what is important in his thought is that Black people do not play a prominent role. This of course, says one or two things: 1) Black people are truly obsolete or 2) Whatever changes that are forecasted will come and Black participation is insignificant. Well, what else is new?. We must take the future into our own hands and disregard the slots others have cast us in. To Mr. Naisbitt's credit he does forecast a form of cultural diversity and sees the rapid increase in the population of Blacks and Spanish speaking Americans as important. Numbers alone will not eradicate racism and economic exploitation and until these sores are cured in the hearts and minds of the white majority, Black participation in the decision making processes that affect them will not materialize. Mr. Naisbitt does give the reader a new way of looking at the future of America and the world. As a social forecaster he is must reading, his chapters on the Information Society, High-Tech/High Touch, World Economy, Institutional Help/Self Help, and North/South should be required reading for all Black people. If his projections are true their impact on us will have a lasting affect.

Witold Rybczynski in his book, **Paper Heroes: A Review of Appropriate Technology**, differentiates between two views of technology: technology as evolutionary and revolutionary. "The former proposes technology as a stepping stone to modernization, the later suggests a new kind of technology with different social and technological goals". Mr. Rybczynski feels that "technological change is not a precondition for social reform." Conversely, he states that social reform can direct technology into more humane areas. Our challenge in the United States, the most technological of societies, is not to be reduced to guinea pigs and play things for scientists. To survive and develop in the last quarter of the 20th century will require a far greater effort than that which has been given over the last twenty-five years. Many say that we are in over our heads, and that there is no hope. I doubt it. We just have to **Learn how to Learn** and seek new knowledge like we seek good times.

XIII

TAKING HOLD OF SELF AND WORLD

The lone individual can only do so much in a capitalistic and technological society. The restrictions are seven fold for the Black individual. Taking hold of one's life **is not an easy task** especially in a culture that, is anti-life and where the existence of negative options are pervasive. First, it is clear that one needs to adopt a perspective that works for rather than against life; for Black people an **Afrocentric*** worldview is best, mainly because such a view starts with the self as a widening center and reaches for knowledge that will allow one to become a stronger, better informed and functioning Black person.

* See Afrocentricity: The Theory of Social Change by Molefi Kete Asante, an important document in the developing theory of Black Consciousness.

Another important admission is to acknowledge to self that most of us have not been educated properly. Aspects of life, like choosing a mate, parenting, planning a future, confronting failure and oppression, are dealt with often on purely emotional terms and serious study in these areas are left to so called experts. George W.S. Trow in **Within the Context of No Context** defines the experts in this way; "In the absence of adults, people come to put their trust in **experts**", and "only an expert can deal with a problem."

The works of Alvin Toffler* document the jet like changes of life in the Western world, yet for the individual to really understand the change that is going on about us, he or she will have to be involved in such change knowingly. Recent studies have concluded "that five years out of college, 50 percent of an engineer's knowledge is obsolete. Engineers who have been out of school for more than a few years may be unable to fully understand what their younger colleagues are saying, writing, or proposing." To most people high-technology is a foreign world, and the only way to correct this is through concentrated study.

Those of us who know how have to be lovingly involved in keeping alive the humane traditions of Afro-American culture. The only way that this can be done is through the maintenance of social institutions that impact on people such as the **family, church and schools.** The most important aspect of course, is how we raise our children, the future adults. In a very important book, **The Disappearance of Childhood** by Neil Postman, he looks in on the damage that this anti-child culture is performing on our youth. His position is that this anti-child culture fosters such nonsense as children as "mini-adults" which puts on the child a world that he or she is not prepared for.

* See Toffler's *Future Shock* and *The Third Wave*.

He also notes that after the collapse of Rome, four factors occurred that are re-emerging in today's cultures: (1) literacy disappeared; (2) education ceased and the little education that existed was not effective; (3) shame disappeared, an important concept, for he sees shame as an integral part of childhood development. In fact he feels that childhood cannot exist without a well-developed idea of shame; (4) as a result of the other three, childhood disappears. His argument rests on the loss of moral directives taught by intelligent and caring adults (parents, teachers, etc.).

Our challenge is not an easy one, life remains a series of potholes and sliding boards. However, we must live and bring life to the world. Here are some suggestions:

(1) As social beings, life is not complete unless we can share the good things with others. Continuity and stability are essential to well being. The family—man, woman, children and extended members, still represent the best structure for early development and re-enforcement of values. A wise people will defy the directives of a throw away and destructive culture and keep the family going, especially if there are children. Remember, the life force that rebuilds all is **love**, seek love and give it especially to your children. Life is not all seriousness and battles; learn to laugh and play. It is unhealthy to be critical and analytical all of the time; relax—have fun and do those things that bring you joy and peace. Laughter heals.

(2) We need formal and informal study. Serious study should be lifelong and structured. Knowledge is one of the few possessions that is difficult to take from a person. View the world as your university and instill in those that you interact with the concept for liberated intellectualism. Develop a basic knowledge

about what is happening in the world. Serious study produces positive and varied options for the individual. Travel whenever possible, try to experience other people and other cultures. Study also gives us the confidence needed to confront problems, the more we understand a problem the better we are able to deal with it. To know is to confront the difficult.

(3) Move toward preventive health. Watch food intake, study nutrition and try to eliminate junk and processed foods. Reduce, and if possible, eliminate meat from the diet. Look into vegetarianism. Avoid alcohol, drugs, cigarettes and all outside negative stimuli. Exercise daily and try to avoid constant mental stress. Seek those aspects of life that are closest to nature, e.g., vegetarianism, clean air, water, sunshine, etc. Seek quality time for yourself, family and friends. Look into meditation as a process of self peace-giving. Basic values are often inward and only need to be activated. Learn to listen to your own silences. True and lasting knowledge occurs when we can become whole from within. People are more than mind, body, and emotions—people are spiritual and to touch one's true self requires the silent investigation of one's deepest core. Wholeness and happiness start with good health and knowing that we have in us the ability to self heal. Do not run from love—seek it and give it. Seek harmony in this world.

(4) Involve yourself in or help develop small cooperative communities to help insulate one against large, impersonal, combative and competitive cities. These self-help cooperatives should use a collective decision making model when possible. People need to be able to make decisions about their lives. Economic models of self-help groups should also be looked upon as an

alternative to forever selling your labor to strangers.

(5) Think well of yourself. Respect the good and encourage the best in all of your contacts. **Discourage gossip and smallness in yourself and others**. Go back to kindness and manners that pull the positive out of people. Be self-activating. Self-actualized people are often able to stimulate their creative sides more often than others through allowing themselves to reach their potential in many life giving areas. Avoid negative emotions such as hate, self-hate as well as hate directed toward others limit growth options.

(6) Try to give quality time on a weekly basis to organized Black struggle in your local area; such as National Black United Front, National Black Independent Political Party, Nation of Islam, SCLC, NAACP, Operation PUSH, church organizations, etc. There are people worldwide who are working day and night to stop our future.

(7) In this anti-life culture small minds rule. People are too willing to accept the negative about others without examination of the criticism of their own hearts. It is that we listen to the destruction of others because of the destruction within us? **Do not lose idealism and vision**, yet maintain realistic expectations of others and self. Finally, stop underestimating the intelligence of others be they women, men, or children.

Within dust and dirt, under voices broadcasting garbage and confusion there is beauty in the world. Do not allow the failures of friend or foe to stop your dreams. The world is a difficult place to negotiate, no one promised an easy fight and if they did, they lied.

IX

Shaping The Future

A people that will be **is**, and a people that was **will rise again**. We must again think and flow in generations. We are the first people. Thousands and thousands of years of history, of timeless and enduring strengths connect us to forces unexplainable. Nations have been built and rebuilt on the knowledge that has been stolen from us. Black people cover the earth like no other, people. Can you imagine what would happen if a simple message of **Liberation** was set in motion—traveling with the speed of light and the patience of the turtle from Afrika to Brazil, from Asia to North America—from Black Point to Black Point?

New seeds have to be planted and this is not an overnight process. A new and enduring **inner autonomy** has to be developed in each and every living Black soul. This inner autonomy (liberation) is our first and most powerful weapon because it is built upon the millions of Black souls who refused to sell their values for golden rocks, positions of status or fake beauty. **Think generations. Think about rebuilding the foundation that built the world.** Just because we are removed from the homeland of our foreparents does not mean defeat or retreat. It's just a greater challenge to show the world what we are made of. The only way to stop future Jonestowns is to create responsible brothers and sisters who will not fall prey to every ego-maniac that comes along with a creative line.

How do you measure a people's existence? You look at their children and then you search out their creations. You survey their art, music, literature, film, drama, and crafts. You investigate their science and look for the results of their technology. You examine their institutions and observe their will to defend themselves against all odds. You measure their ability to show tenderness, exhibit moments of kindness and you always look for the **smile.** The big heart, the enduring "inner force" can be seen in the smile and will radiate from their eyes. A people with vision and purpose will have eyes that shine and glow with future. **The tomorrow that we work and hope for will not only be found in the teachings of our foreparents but will beam incessantly from the eyes of the children. A people who do not see their children as priority are a doomed people. A people who do not protect and prepare their children are a foolish people who are not worthy of greatness or respect from anyone.** A people who see ultimate value in the **acquisition of things** as opposed to the search and enactment of truth through themselves and their children are without a doubt a people who will forever live as slaves.

The Black people that deny themselves their memory, their history (which is the beginning history of the world) are destined to travel the world as barter—and all the peoples of the earth will use and abuse them at will. The secret to any people's greatness is in their self-knowledge—past and present. Only then can the future even be contemplated. We are not only history's creation—we are the creators of history. The enemy's ultimate strength is in the breaking of the spirit through the dispersion of confusion and the inducement of self-doubt. Therefore, we have to cover each others' weaknesses and work toward the re-enforcement of one another's strengths.

A people that take the time to turn off television sets, open dusty and unread books, form study groups, create children and food coops, understand the importance of land; but most importantly, a people who move toward critical **self-examination** are then and only then worthy of a self-determining destiny. Show me a man or woman that has **seriously** studied the history of his/her people and I will show you a serious brother or sister; I will show you a person who takes rather than begs, creates rather than destroys, leads rather than follows, initiates rather than copies; I will show you a people who have created moral laws based on the practice of truth and justice. I will show you a people who will outlive time and blow dust into the eyes of the excuse-makers. I will show you a people who are elder-conscious and children-blessed. I will show you a people that **will be, is,** and **will rise again. I will show you Black people whose re-entrance into the world will be one that emphasizes memory and development and whose rallying cry will be REMEMBER THE MIDDLE PASSAGE.**

Afterword

by
Darwin T. Turner

Earthquakes and Sun Rise Missions is Haki R. Madhubuti's first volume of poetry since **Book of Life** (1973). Although he has continued to write poerty during this decade, the effort to publish it has submitted to other priorities—arduous work as the director of the Institute of Positive Education and of Third World Press, three books of essays, continuing his work as educator and nation builder, and the responsibilities of a husband and a father. Now the poet has reappeared in a volume of rich love of Black women, mature, compassionate observation, and cold contempt of the enemies of Black people.

Under the name "Don L. Lee", Madhubuti published his first books of poetry in the late 1960s as part of a generation of young Black writers using their skills to educate Black people to a heightened Black consciousness. Introducing his first collection of poems, **Think Black**, (1967), he wrote,

Black art will elevate and enlighten our people and lead them toward an awareness of self, i.e., their blackness. It will show them mirrors. Beautiful symbols. And will aid in the destruction of anything nasty and detrimental to our advancement as a people.

But, as Dudley Randall asserted in an introduction to Madhubuti's second collection, **Black Pride** (1968),

...it is not his recital of received pieties which makes him a poet. Don Lee is a poet because of his resourcefulness with language. He writes for the man in the streeet, and uses the language of the street...with, inventiveness, and surprise... (He) joins words together or splits syllables into fractions for greater expressiveness. His shorter lyrics have a sting and his longer poems a force that make him one of the most interesting of the revolutionary young black poets.

In an essay published in **A Capsule Course In Black Poetry Writing** (1975), Madhubuti wrote:

Originality for the Black poet essentially means you must either have something new and insightful to say...or you must find a new way of saying something that has already been said...- Such themes as the **fact** that Europeans are bent on destroying Afrikan peoples, that the black middle class often copies the styles and values of Europeans and that Afrikan peoples' need to get together, are not original...Thus,if you choose to deal with such themes (and they must be dealt with), you **must** create a form/style which is original, which is not a copy of other poets.

Don't Cry, Scream (1970), his third collection of

poems, brilliantly illustrates his advice. Improving as rapidly as Randall had predicted and growing beyond the introspection of his early poems, Madhubuti focused on themes and subjects that characterize his thought but are not new: satiric denunciations of games-players who do not comprehend Blackness ("But he was Cool/or: he even stopped for green lights," "Malcolm Spoke/who listened?"); impassioned exhortations for heightened Black consciousness ("A Poem to Complement Other Poems"); reverence for Blacks who commit their lives and work to Black people ("Gwendolyn Brooks," "Don't Cry, Scream—for John Coltrane/from a black poet/in a basement apt. crying dry tears of 'you ain't gone.'"); and love for Black women and Black children ("A Poem Looking for a Reader/to be read with a love consciousness," "A Message All Black people can Dig/& a few negroes too.)

What gave originality to these important but familiar subjects and themes was only partly Madhubuti's startling metaphors ("his wine didn't have to be cooled, him was air conditioned cool...so cool him nick-named refrigerator") and his unexpected twists of thought ("him wanted to be a TV star. him is. ten o'clock news./wanted, wanted. nigger stole some lemon & lime popsicles, thought them were diamonds.") Even more originally, however, he used word sound and staccato repetition with a skill that justifies Gwendolyn Brooks' praise in her introduction to **Don't Cry, Scream**: "At the hub of the new wordway is Don Lee." At times, he strained to overcome the limitations of the printed words by creating sound that artistically would evoke emotion. Demanding to be read aloud, his poetry in his third volume sometimes suggests the virtuoso efforts of jazz singers who use their human voices to replicate the sounds of musical instruments. For example, consider a passage from the title poem of **Don't Cry Scream:**

Trane done went.
(got his hat & left me one)
naw brother,
i didn't cry,
i just—
Scream-eeeeeeeeeeeeeee-ed   sing loud
SCREAM-EEEEEEEEEEEEEEEEE-ED & high with
we-eeeeeeeeeeeeeeeeeeeeeeee   feeling
WE-EEEEEEeeeeeeeeeEEEEEEEE   letting
WE-EEEEEEEEEEEEEEEEEEEEEEE   yr/voice
WHERE YOU DONE GONE, BROTHER?
                                   break

Equally powerful is his use of repetition. In his essay in **A Capsule Course in Black Poetry Writing,** Madhubuti praised Amiri Baraka's artistic creation of black music rhythms through the repetition of "stressed sounds at intervals that are dictated by his feel for black liferhythms and blackmusic." Perhaps this is equally valid as an explanation of Madhubuti's style, but I do not believe that it is the complete explanation. Madhubuti's artistry conceals itself. In contrast to Baraka who, in such a poem as "Beautiful Black Women", seems to be manipulating metaphor and sound consciously as he leads a reader from an image of Black women weeping to am image of rain to a thought that Black women should not be weeping but should be queens who reign, Madhubuti seems at first merely to be repeating words. Unexpectedly, however, the repetition develops its own rhythm; and often the reader becomes conscious of a new message just as, when one is lazily listening to stereo, one may suddenly become aware of hearing a different theme from a second speaker. Consider the following examples, from "A Poem to Complement Other Poems",

change nigger change.
know the realenemy.
change: is us is or is u aint. change. now now
   change. for the better.
   read a change. live a change. read a
      blackpoem.
   change. be the realpeople.
   change. blackpoems
will change:
know the realenemy. change. know the real-
      enemy.
   change yr/enemy change know the real
change know the realenemy change, change,
      know the
   realenemy, the realenemy, the real
realenemy change your the enemies/change
      change
   your change your enemy change
your enemy. know the realenemy, the world's
      enemy.
   know them know them know them the
realenemy change change your enemy change
      your change
   change change your enemy change change
change change your change change change.
your
mind nigger.

and from "Gwendolyn Brooks"

   into the sixties
   a word was born.....BLACK
   & with black came poets
   & from the poet's ball points came:
   black doubleblack purpleblack blueblack been-
      black was
   black daybeforeyesterday blackerthan ultrablack
      super

black blackblack yellowblack niggerblack black-
whi-teman
blackerthanyoueverbes 1/4 black unblack cold-
black clear
black my momma's blackerthanyour momma
pimpleblack fall
black so black we can't even see you black on
black in
black by black technically black mantanblack
winter
black coolblack 360degreesblack coalblack midnight
black black when it's convenient rustyblack
moonblack
black starblack summerblack electronblack
spaceman
black shoeshineblack jimshoeblack underwear-
black ugly
black auntjimammablack, uncleben's rice black
williebest
black blackisbeautifulblack i justdiscoveredblack
negro
black unsubstanceblack.

We Walk the Way of the New World (1970) and
Directionscore (1971) resonate and expand earlier
themes: the unity of Blacks throughout the world, the
love of Black women, and the vision of a new world.
Three years later **Book of Life** suggests a change in
poetic concept and style. In Part I, Madhubuti
continued to use the familiar style to assail
"traitors"—Blacks who, having profited individually,
jumped from the train of revolution or even tried to
impede further progress—and to exhort Blacks to
continue to move toward a new day. In Part II,
however, the poet's voice—no less determined than
before—is quieter, more contemplative, more re-
strained. Abandoning slashing satire (which on oc-

casion perhaps dissipated some of the seriousness of its criticism by provoking laughter), Madhubuti criticized through thoughtful aphorisms:

56

We do not equate
poverty with blackness
nor do we equate the lavish
use of wealth with blackness.
we now live in a time
where the many go without
while for the few we have entrusted to lead us
luxuries have become needs

Instead of dramatically proclaiming the need for a new world, he quietly urged people to think about life:

53

How many of our children
have seen the ocean's ripple
or have felt the morning wetness
of country
vegetation
or picked the just ripened fruit from trees
or enjoyed the afternoon sun bathing
their bodies as they played in the green.

there is little that is green in the cities
other than the broken stop lights and
artificial grass.
our children's dreams are lost among the
concrete of too many promises
waiting for elevators to take them
to the top floors of public housing.

Perhaps, in a sense, the change reflected his effort to follow his own observation:

best teachers
seldom teach
they be and do.

Now, a decade later, an older, quieter voice
seems to control the poetry of **Earthquakes and Sun
Rise Missions**. It is as though Madhubuti has chosen
to move from the role of virtuoso performer and to
assume more often the role of artistic, prophetic
educator. Madhubuti has not abandoned the earlier
style, which he continues to display in such poems as
"Negro Leaderships", "Rainforest", "We Struggle for
the People", or "destiny"; but now he often seeks to
fuse poetry and prose, as in "Woman Black" or
'Winterman", for example. He has not forsaken his
stern criticism of Blacks who pursue false values, but
he now also writes compassionately of the reasons
some do ("Winterman"). There is an increased emphasis on a message of love for Black women, but
there is continuing evidence of love for and commitment to Black people. As Gwendolyn Brooks wrote in
the introduction to **Don't Cry, Scream**, "Around a
black audience he puts warm hands."

More than a decade ago, while teachers in
schools were complaining about students' lack of
interest in poetry, Madhubuti was proving that people
will listen to and buy poetry that speaks to them, that
entertains and educates them. Now, concerned that
some poets have lost their vision and that other poets'
voices have been drowned by the sounds from the
ever-present television sets, he is reaching out poeti-
cally once more to urge people to listen,

We can do what we work to do.
measure stillness and quiet
noise is ever present.
if we are not careful we will not

hear the message
when it
arrives.

Madhubuti's powerful message will shut off some television sets, redirect some minds and may invite book burning in some quarters.

SELECTED BIBLIOGRAPHY

History

Barraclough, Geoffrey. *Main Trends in History.* New York, 1978. *Turning Points in World History.* New York, 1979.

Ben-Jochannan, Yosef. *The Saga of the "Black Marxist" versus "The Black Nationalist", A Debate Resurrected.* New York, 1978. Dr. Ben-Jochannan has published over twelve books in the area of Black history, Theology and Political thought; I strongly suggest that the reader investigate all of his works.

Bennett, Lerone, Jr. *The Challenge of Blackness.* Chicago, 1972. *The Shape of Black America.* Chicago, 1975.

Berlin, Isaiah. *Against the Current.* England, 1979.

Bradley, Michael. *The Iceman Inheritance.* Toronto, 1978.

Cruse, Harold. *The Crisis of the Negro Intellectual.* New York, 1967.

Diop, Cheikh Anta. *The Cultural Unity of Black Africa* Chicago, 1978. *The African Origin of Civilization: Myth or Reality.* New York, 1974.

Harding, Vincent. *There is a River.* New York, 1981.

Jackson, John G. *Introduction to African Civilizations.* New York, 1970. *Man, God, and Civilization.* New York, 1972.

Jones, James H. *Bad Blood: The Tuskegee Syphilis Experiment.* New York, 1981.

Kiernan, V.G. *America: The New Imperialism: From White Settlement to World Hegemony.* London, 1980.

Moses, Wilson Jeremiah. *The Golden Age of Black Nationalism 1850-1925.* Hamden, 1978.

Mosse, George L. *Toward the Final Solution: A History of European Racism.* New York, 1978.

Oakes, James. *The Ruling Race.* New York, 1982.

Parry, J.H. *The Establishment of the European Hegemony: 1415-1715.* New York, 1966.

Van Sertima, Ivan. *They Came Before Columbus.* New York, 1976.

Williams, Chancellor. *The Destruction of Black Civilization: Great Issues of A Race From 4500 B.C. to 2000 A.D.* Chicago, 1974.

Williams, William Appleman. *Empire As A Way Of Life.* New York, 1980.

Zinn, Howard. *A People's History of the United States.* New York, 1980.

Power, Politics, Economics and War

Chace, James. *Solvency: The Price of Survival.* New York, 1981.

Domhoff, William G. *The Powers That Be: Processes of Ruling Class Domination in America.* New York, 1978.

Fallows, James. *National Defense.* New York, 1981.

Franck, Thomas M., Weisband, Edward., Eds. *Secrecy and Foreign Policy.* London, 1974.

Jacobs, Jane. *The Question of Separatism: Quebec and the Struggle Over Sovereignty.* New York, 1980.

Jencks, Christopher. *Who Gets Ahead?, The Determinants of Success in America.* New York, 1979.

Lekachman, Robert. *Greed Is Not Enough: Reaganomics.* New York, 1982.

Nyberg, David. *Power Over Power.* Ithaca, 1981.

Rapoport, Anatol, Ed. *Clausewitz on War.* England, 1974.

Stein, Arthur A. *The Nation At War.* Baltimore, 1978.

Waterlow, Charlotte. *Superpowers and Victims: The Outlook For World Community.* Englewood Cliffs, 1974.

RELIGION

Ben-Jochannan, Yosef. A. A. *Our Black Seminarians and Black Clergy Without A Black Theology.* New York, 1978.

Cleage, Albert B., Jr. *Black Christian Nationalism.* New York, 1972.

Cone, James. *Liberation : A Black Theology of Liberation.* New York, 1970.

Conway, Flo and Siegelman, Jim. *Snapping.* New York, 1978.

Frazier, E. Franklin and Lincoln, C. Eric. *The Negro Church in America* and *The Black Church Since Frazier*. New York, 1974.

Konolige, Frederica and Konolige, Kit. *The Power of Their Glory:-America's Ruling Class: The Espiscopalians*. New York, 1974.

Perkins, Staunton E. Smith. *Satan in the Pulpit*. Rocky Mount, 1981.

Raboteau, Albert J. *Slave Religion*. New York, 1978.

Tendzin, Osel. *Buddha in the Palm of Your Hand*. Boulder, 1981.

Washington, Joseph R., Jr. *The Politics of God*. Boston, 1970.

PSYCHOLOGY, MIND CONTROL AND INTELLIGENCE

Akbar, Na'im. *Mental Disorder Among African-Americans*. Black Books Bulletin, Vol. 7., no. 2, Chicago, 1981.

Chavkin, Samuel. *The Mind Stealers: Psychosurgery and Mind Control*. Boston, 1978.

Chorover, Stephan L. *From Genisis to Genocide*. Cambridge, 1979.

Guthrie, Robert V. *Even The Rat Was White*. New York, 1976.

Gould, Stephen Jay. *The Mismeasure of Man*. New York, 1981.

Herrnstein, R.J., I.Q. Testing and the Media. *The Atlantic* August, 1982.

Jones, Reginald L. Ed. *Black Psychology*. New York, 1980.

Key, Wilson Bryan. *Subliminal Seduction*. New York, 1972.

Schiller, Herbert I. *The Mind Managers*. Boston, 1973.

Schrag, Peter. *Mind Control*. New York, 1978.

Skinner, B.F. *Beyond Freedom and Dignity*. New York, 1971.

Szasz, Thomas. *Psychiatric Slavery*. New York, 1977.

Welsing, Frances. Interview in *Black Books, Bulletin,* Vol. 6, No. 4., Chicago, 1980. "The Color of God", *Black Books Bulletin,* Vol. 7, No. 1., Chicago, 1980.

Wright, Bobby. "Black Suicide: Lynching By Any Other Name is Still Lynching. *Black Books Bulletin*. Vol. 7, No. 2., Chicago 1981.

MEDIA

Cirino, Robert. *Don't Blame The People*. New York, 1971.

Copaine, Benjamin M., Ed. *Who Owns The Media?* New York, 1979.

Mander, Jerry. *Four Arguments For the Elimination of Television*. New York, 1978.

Rosenblum, Mort. *Coups and Earthquakes: Reporting The World To America*. New York, 1981.

Said, Edward W. *Covering Islam*. New York, 1981.

Swerdlow, Joel and Mankiewicz, Frank. *Remote Control: Television And the Manipulation of American Life*. New York, 1978.

Smith, Anthony. *The Geopolitics of Information: How Western Culture Dominates The World*. New York, 1978.

Tuchman, Gaye. *Making News*. New York, 1978.

JAPAN

Musashi, Miyamoto. Translated by Victor Harris. *A Book Of Five Rings*. New York, 1982.

Najita, Tetsuo. *Japan: The Intellectual Foundations of Modern Japanese Politics*. Chicago, 1974.

Tsunetomo, Yamamoto. Translated by William Scott Wilson. *The Book of The Samurai*. New York, 1979.

Vogel, Ezra F. *Japan As Number 1: Lessons for America*. New York, 1979.

CRIME

Blackstock, Nelson. *Cointelpro*. New York, 1976.

Bryce, Herrington J., Ed. *Black Crime: A Police View*. Washington, 1977.

Currie, Elliott. Fighting Crime, *Working Papers*. Cambridge, July-August, 1982.

Geis, Gilbert and Meier, Robert F. *White-Collar Crime*. New York, 1977.

Kwitny, Jonathan. *Vicious Circles: The Mafia in the Market Place*. New York, 1977.

MacNamara, Donald E.J. and Sagarin, Edward. *Sex, Crime and the Law.* New York, 1971.

Neely, Richard. "The Politics of Crime". *The Atlantic Monthly.* 1982.

Perkus, Cathy, Ed. *Cointelpro: The FBI's Secret War On Political Freedom.* New York, 1975.

Plate, Thomas and Darvi, Andrea. *Secret Police.* Garden City, 1981.

Silberman, Charles E. *Criminal Violence, Criminal Justice.* New York, 1980.

CHILDREN AND EDUCATION

Copperman, Paul. *The Literacy Hoax.* New York, 1980.

Cornoy, Martin. *Education As Cultural Imperialism.* New York, 1974.

de Lone, Richard H. *Small Futures.* New York, 1979.

Kozol, Jonathan. *Prisoners of Silence.* New York, 1980.

Postman, Neil. *The Disappearance of Childhood.* New York, 1982.

Townsend, Peter. *The Smallest Pawns in the Game.* Boston, 1980.

CONTEMPORARY POLITICS

Asnate, Molefi Kete. *Afrocentricity: The Theory of Social Change.* Buffalo, 1980.

de la Boetie, Etienne. *The Politics of Obedience: The Discourse of Voluntary Servitude.* New York, 1975.

Gill, Gerald R. *Meanness Mania: The Changed Mood.* Washington, 1980.

Glasgow, Douglas G. *The Black Underclass.* New York, 1981.

Hacker, Andrew. "The Lower Depths". *New York Review of Books.* August 12, 1982.

Marable, Manning, *From The Grassroots.* Boston, 1980.

Robertson, Wilmot. *The Dispossessed Majority.* Cape Canaveral, 1973.

Ronen, Dov. *The Quest for Self Determination.* New Haven, 1979.

Ryan, William *Equality*. New York, 1981.

Sennett, Richard. *Authority*. New York, 1980.

TECHNOLOGY AND SURVIVALISM

Colin, Norman. *The God That Limps: Science and Technology in the Eighties*. New York, 1981.

Giehl, Dudley. *Vegetarianism: A Way of Life*. New York, 1979.

Hawken, Ogilvy and Schwartz. *Seven Tomorrows*. New York, 1982.

McGee, Charles T. *How to Survive Modern Technology*. Alamo, 1979.

Naisbitt, John. *Megatrends: Ten New Directions Transforming Our Lives*. New York, 1982.

Rybczynski, Witold. *Paper Heroes: A Review of Appropriate Technology*. New York, 1980.

Schell, Jonathan. *The Fate of the Earth*. New York, 1982.

Schumacher, E.F. *Small is Beautiful*. New York, 1977.

Tappan, Mel. *Tappan on Survival*. Rogue River, 1981.

CULTURE: ANTHROPOLOGY AND SOCIOLOGY

Counter, S. Allen and Evans, David L. *I Sought My Brother*. Cambridge, 1981.

Gans, Herbert J. *Popular Culture and High Culture*. New York, 1974.

Hall, Edward T. *Beyond Culture*. Garden City, 1976.

Harris, Marvin. *America Now: The Anthropology of a Changing Culture*. New York, 1981. *Cultural Materialism: The Struggle for a Science of Culture*. New York, 1974. *Cows, Pigs, Wars and Witches: The Riddle of Culture*. New York, 1974.

Karenga, Maulana. *Introduction to Black Studies*. Inglewood, 1982. *Essays on Struggle: Position and Analysis*. Inglewood, 1979. *Kwanzaa: Origins, Concepts, Practice*. Inglewood, 1977. *Kawaida Theory*. Inglewood, 1980.

Lewis, Michael. *The Culture of Inequality*. New York, 1978.

Mead, Margaret. *And Keep Your Power Dry.* New York, 1965.

Swartz, Marc J. and Jordan, David K. *Culture: The Anthropological Perceptive.* New York, 1980.

White, Leslie A. *The Science of Culture.* New York, 1969.

MALE-FEMALE RELATIONSHIPS

Janssen-Jurreit. *Sexism: The Male Monopoly in History and Thought.* New York, 1982.

Langley, Roger and Levy, Richard C. *Wife Beating: The Silent Crisis.* New York, 1977.

Lips, Hilary M. *Women, Men and the Psychology of Power.* Englewood Cliffs, 1981.

McAdoo, Harriette Piper, Ed. *Black Families.* Beverly Hills, 1981.

Maccoby, Eleanor Emmons and Jouclin, Carol Nagy. *The Psychology of Sex Differences.* Stanford, 1974.

Mead, Margaret. *Male and Female: A Study of the Sexes in a Changing World.* New York, 1949.

Rodgers-Rose, LaFrances, Ed. *The Black Woman.* Beverly Hills, 1980.

Sunday, Peggy Reeves. *Female Power and Male Dominance.* Cambridge, 1981.

Staples, Robert. *Black Masculinity: The Black Male's Role In American Society.* San Francisco, 1982. *The Black Woman in America.* Chicago, 1976. *The World of Black Singles.* Westport, 1981.

Ya Salaam, Kalamu. *Our Women Keep Our Skies From Falling.* Orleans, 1980.

About the Author and Other Contributors

Haki R. Madhubuti is the Director of the Institute of Positive Education and Editor of Third World Press. The author of sixteen books of poetry, literary criticism, and essays, he has been poet - in- residence at Cornell University, Howard University, Central State University, and the University of Illinois - Circle Campus. He is the recipient of awards from the Illinois Arts Council and the National Endowment for the Arts. Recently his work has been highlighted on *CBS News Nightwatch,* National Public Radio's *All Things Considered, The Washington Post, The New York Times, Essence* magazine, *The Chicago Tribune, The MacNeil/Lehrer News Hour, America's Black Forum,* and Black Entertainment Television.

His published books are *Think Black* (1967), *Black Pride* (1968), *Don't Cry, Scream* (1969), *We Walk the Way of the New World* (1970), *Directionscore : Selected and New Poems* (1971), *To Gwen, With Love* edited with Francis Ward and Patricia L. Brown (1971), *Dynamite Voices: Black Poets of the 1960's* (1971), *Kwanzaa: A Progressive and Uplifting African-American Holiday* (1972), *From Plan To Planet* (1973), *Book of Life* (1973), *A Capsule Course in Black Poetry Writing* co-authored with Gwendolyn Brooks, Keorapetse Kgositsile and Dudley Randall (1975), *Enemies:The Clash of Races* (1978), *Earthquakes and Sunrise Missions* (1984), *Killing Memory, Seeking Ancestors* (1987), *Say That the River Turns: The Impact of Gwendolyn Brooks* (1987) and *Black Men: Obsolete, Single Dangerous? The Afrikan American Family in Transition* (1990).

Mr. Madhubuti earned his MFA from the University of Iowa and is a professor of English at Chicago State University. He lives in Chicago with his wife and children.

Darwin Turner is chairman of the Afro-American Studies Department at the University of Iowa. He has edited, authored, and contributed to many books, articles, and reviews on authors from Dunbar to Hawthorne to Baldwin. He has researched and written extensively on the published and unpublished works of Jean Toomer. His latest book is *The Wayward and the Seeking: A Collection of Writings by Jean Toomer.*

Calvin Jones is a Chicago painter, muralist, illustrator, and long standing member of the National Conference of Artists. He was a participant in FESTAC and is listed in Who's Who of American Artists and Who's Who of Black American Artists. His work is internationally respected and he is widely known for his unselfish contributions to Black struggle and advancement.

ALSO AVAILABLE FROM THIRD WORLD PRESS

Nonfiction

*The Destruction Of Black
Civilization: Great Issues
Of A Race From 4500 B.C.
To 2000 A.D.*
by Dr. Chancellor Williams
paper $16.95
cloth $29.95

*The Cultural Unity Of
Black Africa*
by Cheikh Anta Diop $14.95

Home Is A Dirty Street
by Useni Eugene Perkins $9.95

*Black Men: Obsolete, Single,
Dangerous?*
by Haki R. Madhubuti
paper $14.95
cloth $29.95

*From Plan To Planet
Life Studies: The Need
For Afrikan Minds And
Institutions*
by Haki R. Madhubuti $7.95

Enemies: The Clash Of Races
by Haki R. Madhubuti $12.95

*Kwanzaa: A Progressive And
Uplifting African-American
Holiday*
by Institute of Positive Education
Intro. by Haki R. Madhubuti $2.50

*Harvesting New Generations:
The Positive Development Of
Black Youth*
by Useni Eugene Perkins $12.95

*Explosion Of Chicago
Black Street Gangs*
by Useni Eugene Perkins $6.95

*The Psychopathic Racial
Personality And Other Essays*
by Dr. Bobby E. Wright $5.95

*Black Women, Feminism And Black
Liberation: Which Way?*
by Vivian V. Gordon $5.95

Black Rituals
by Sterling Plumpp $8.95

*The Redemption Of Africa
And Black Religion*
by St. Clair Drake $6.95

How I Wrote Jubilee
by Margaret Walker $1.50

A Lonely Place Against The Sky
by Dorothy Palmer Smith $7.95

Fiction

*Mostly Womenfolk And A Man
Or Two: A Collection*
by Mignon Holland Anderson $5.95

The Brass Bed and Other Stories
Pearl Cleage $8.00

Poetry and Drama

To Disembark
by Gwendolyn Brooks $6.95

I've Been A Woman
by Sonia Sanchez $7.95

My One Good Nerve
by Ruby Dee $8.95

Geechies
by Gregory Millard $5.95

Earthquakes And Sunrise Missions
by Haki R. Madhubuti $8.95

Killing Memory: Seeking Ancestors
by Haki R. Madhubuti $8.00

Say That The River Turns:
The Impact Of Gwendolyn Brooks
(Anthology)
Ed.by Haki R. Madhubuti $8.95

Octavia And Other Poems
by Naomi Long Madgett $8.00

A Move Further South
by Ruth Garnett $7.95

Manish
by Alfred Woods $8.00

New Plays for the Black Theatre
(Anthology)
edited by Woodie King, Jr. $14.95

Children's Books

The Day They Stole
The Letter J
by Jabari Mahiri $3.95

The Tiger Who Wore
White Gloves
by Gwendolyn Brooks $5.00

A Sound Investment
by Sonia Sanchez $2.95

I Look At Me
by Mari Evans $2.50

Black Books Bulletin

A limited number of back issues
of this unique journal are available
at $3.00 each:

Vol. 1, Fall '71   Interview with
                    Hoyt W. Fuller

Vol. 1, No. 3   Interview with
                    Lerone Bennett, Jr.

Vol. 5, No. 3   Science & Struggle

Vol. 5, No. 4   Blacks & Jews

Vol. 7, No. 3   The South

Order from **Third World Press**
7524 S. Cottage Grove Ave.
Chicago, IL 60619

Shipping: Add $2.00 for first book
and .25 for each additional book.
Mastercard /Visa orders may be placed
by calling 1-312/651-0700